DIVINE IMAGES

DIVINE

A HISTORY OF JESUS

IMAGES

ON THE SCREEN

by Roy Kinnard and Tim Davis

A Citadel Press Book
Published by Carol Publishing Group

Copyright © 1992 by Roy Kinnard and Tim Davis

A Citadel Press Book
Published by Carol Publishing Group
Citadel Press is a registered trademark of
Carol Communications, Inc.

Editorial Offices   Sales & Distribution Offices
600 Madison Avenue   120 Enterprise Avenue
New York, NY 10022   Secaucus, NJ 07094

In Canada: Canadian Manda Group
P.O. Box 920, Station U
Toronto, Ontario M8Z 5P9

Queries regarding rights and permissions
should be addressed to: Carol Publishing Group,
600 Madison Avenue, New York, NY 10022

Manufactured in the United States of America
10 9 8 7 6 5 4 3 2 1

Carol Publishing Group books are available at special discounts
for bulk purchases, for sales promotions, fund raising, or
educational purposes. Special editions can also be created to
specifications. For details contact: Special Sales Department,
Carol Publishing Group, 120 Enterprise Ave., Secaucus, NJ 07094

Designed by A. Christopher Simon

Cataloging data for this title may be obtained from the
Library of Congress.

ISBN 0-8065-1284-9

for
Dot and E. L.
and for
Keith

ACKNOWLEDGMENTS

The authors would like to thank the following individuals, whose contributions were essential to the completion of this book:

Tony Clay; John Cocchi; Tony Crnkovich; Rose Crnkovich; Barbara Puorro Galasso and Jan Christopher-Horak of George Eastman House; Irving Lippman; Alvin H. Marill; Rob McKay; Emily Meehan; Eileen McMahon of Tribune Entertainment; Dana Miller of Turner Network Television; Jerry Ohlinger; Fred Palkovics; Linda Pototsky of the American Film Institute, John F. Kennedy Center, Washington, D. C.; Reg Shrader of the University of Wisconsin, State Historical Society; Veto Stasiunaitus; George Turner of *American Cinematographer* magazine; and our editor at Citadel Press, Allan J. Wilson. Appreciation also goes to the Jerry Vermilye Collection for the use of a number of photos.

CONTENTS

Introduction 13

Chapter 1—The Early Silents (1897–1919) 19

The Passion Play of Oberammergau 19
From the Manger to the Cross 21
Intolerance 22
More Early Silents 27

Chapter 2—The Nineteen Twenties 37

Ben-Hur 37
The King of Kings 40
More Films of the 1920s 45

Chapter 3—The Nineteen Thirties 51

Destination Unknown 51
The Last Days of Pompeii 52
More Films of the 1930s 56

Chapter 4—The Nineteen Forties 59

Strange Cargo 59
The Great Commandment 60
The Lawton Story 62
More Films of the 1940s 65

Chapter 5—The Nineteen Fifties 73

Quo Vadis? 73
I Beheld His Glory 79

Salomé 81
The Robe 84
Demetrius and the Gladiators 89
The Silver Chalice 93
Day of Triumph 95
The Prodigal 103
Celui Qui Doit Mourir (He Who Must Die) 107
Il Maestro (The Teacher and the Miracle) 111
Ordet (The Word) 111
The Big Fisherman 114
Ben-Hur 118
Desert Desperadoes (aka The Sinner) 126
More Films of the 1950s 126

Chapter 6—The Nineteen Sixties 131

King of Kings 131
Whistle Down the Wind 140
Barabbas 145
Ponzio Pilato (Pontius Pilate) 152
The Greatest Story Ever Told 154
Il Vangelo Secondo Matteo (The Gospel According to St. Matthew) 162
Seduto Alla Sur Destra (Black Jesus) 167
La Voie Lactee (The Milky Way) 168
More Films of the 1960s 169

Chapter 7—The Nineteen Seventies 171

Johnny Got His Gun 171

The Ruling Class   173
Gospel Road   175
Godspell   177
Jesus Christ, Superstar   177
The Passover Plot   183
Jesus of Nazareth   185
The Nativity   189
Mary and Joseph: A Story of Faith   191
Monty Python's Life of Brian   192
Jesus   195
More Films of the 1970s   198

Chapter 8—The Nineteen Eighties   201

The Day Christ Died   201
In Search of Historic Jesus   203
Je Vous Salue, Marie (Hail, Mary)   203
The Seventh Sign   205
The Last Temptation of Christ   207
Jesus of Montreal   212
A Child Called Jesus   213
More Films of the 1980s   219

Appendix   221

DIVINE IMAGES

THE PASSION PLAY OF OBERAMMERGAU: Frank Russell (center) as Jesus.

INTRODUCTION

"Who are men saying that I am?"

—MARK 8:27

Who was Jesus of Nazareth? Considering the mighty and enduring impact, the overpowering influence that the teachings of Jesus and the religion based on those teachings have had on society, on the very course of history during the past two thousand years, little factual information is known about the man who started it all. Almost all of the information we do have is culled from the Gospels of Mark, Luke, Matthew, and John in the New Testament; the earliest of these, the more than six hundred-fifty verses of Mark, was recorded c. 70 A.D., about thirty-five to forty years after the Crucifixion. Even the exact historical date of Jesus's birth is not certain; the event has been set at either 6 or 5 B.C., with many placing the date at 11 or 7 B.C., and some maintaining that 4 B.C. is the most likely date, since that is the year King Herod, who feared the prophesied birth of the Saviour, died. (The widespread belief in 1 A.D. as the birthdate did not gain acceptance until the sixth century A.D. when a Russian monk, Dionysius Exiguus, made an erroneous calculation.) The Gospels were written belatedly in reaction to the explosive growth of Christianity; by 60–70 A.D. the religion had become so widespread that the traditional oral communication of the Scriptures was no longer practical.

Since the four Gospels disagree (at times widely) on the exact details of the events they describe and the pronouncements and conversations quoted, those critical of religion sometimes have used this disparity to refute Scriptural veracity. To fundamentalist Christians, every word in the Bible is literally true; to atheists, every word is fable; the truth, no doubt, is somewhere between these two opposites. That Jesus of Nazareth existed is undeniable; the deep resonance, the heartfelt eloquence of the Scriptures, the past, present, and continuing influence of his life on human thought and deed stand as testimony to that fact.

The Bible, for all its textured prose, is nevertheless vague on many details, and the visual, if not the spiritual, concept that most people have of Jesus Christ is derived less from the Gospels than from outside sources such as paintings down through the ages or, in the twentieth century, from film.

Even a cursory look at the films discussed in this book will reveal a striking change in the manner in which Jesus Christ has been portrayed in movies over the course of the twentieth century. This is even more obvious when one focuses on the biblical films that attempt to

13

faithfully reproduce the events described in the New Testament. The once-solemn, stoic, and (lifelessly) reverent portrayal of an all-divine Christ, which audiences demanded and these films provided, have, by virtual necessity, been replaced by more realistic and introspective productions which, for better or worse, explore Jesus, the man who also happened to be God. The reason for this change is twofold, coming about partially because of the social, political, and religious changes since the 1960s, but principally because of the inherent limitations of a narrowly interpreted "divine" characterization. In order to keep the Gospels relevant to a society with changing values, the film portrayals of Jesus have also changed and will in all likelihood continue to do so.

Nearly every title in *Divine Images* acknowledges some derivation or combination of the Gospels as the principal source material for their retelling of Jesus's life. The problem with using the books of Matthew, Mark, Luke, and John, as the creators of these films have often found, is that the Apostles were excellent storytellers but poor screenwriters. Written as inspirational articles of faith first and recorded history second, the Gospels provide their characters with vague motivations and sometimes indistinct personalities. Why did Judas Iscariot betray Jesus? Merely for thirty pieces of silver? How much of a role did the Jewish religious leaders of that time play in Jesus's arrest and Crucifixion? What, exactly, did Jesus experience during his forty-day sojourn in the desert? Who was Salomé, and was she really the instigator responsible for Herod's beheading of John the Baptist? How should a screenwriter adapting this material structure his script? By adapting only one of the Gospels? Which one? Or should the writer attempt to combine the four into a composite? Should any of the more than thirty specific miracles attributed to Jesus in the Gospels be shown? If so, how should these occurrences be visualized—literally or suggestively? These are just a few of the questions that filmmakers have had to address since the 1898 production, *The Passion Play of Oberammergau*, was first screened. Most perplexing of all is that there are no hard details available on the central figure of the Gospels: Jesus. It is for these reasons, among others, that film productions of Jesus's life have been among the most difficult for moviemakers to successfully execute.

As Jesus the elusive historical person has confounded archaeologists and researchers for centuries, so has he confounded and frustrated artists and dramatists intent on capturing his image. The filmmakers of the late nineteenth and early twentieth centuries had nowhere to turn for visual inspiration except the Renaissance-Baroque paintings by the great masters of European art, and it was from this rich iconography that much of the cinematic imagery so familiar to movie audiences was derived; the first simple movie representations of Jesus Christ were adapted from traditional Bible illustrations. Faced with the obvious problems in characterizing someone whose actual personality is totally unknown, and realizing the definite potential of offending audiences and clergy if their personal ideal is not preserved, early filmmakers naturally gravitated to a bland, Sunday-school vision of Christ. Safe, as well as appealing to a mass audience, halo-adorned, blue-eyed, white-robed Boy Scout from Judea became the accepted film version of Jesus for more than sixty years. This picture-postcard ideal of Jesus was so firmly entrenched that *Variety* actually criticized one early film because it dared to show Jesus without a nimbus, the symbolic halo seen in many paintings. With only slight variations, this was the only interpretation of Christ the movies presented until the mid-1960s.

The main drawback to this simplified vision of Jesus is that it leaves us with a totally divine individual virtually impossible to identify with because of his detachment from the rest of humanity. As these film interpretations of Jesus's life maximized the divine and minimized the human qualities, they were eventually unable to draw mass public interest and box-office response. Instead, filmmakers titillated audiences by contrasting the debauchery of the Roman Empire with the glory of Jesus and the faith of his followers. The persecution of early Christians and the orgies of the Roman ruling class received increasing emphasis in each of the succeeding productions of *The Last Days of Pompeii* and *Quo Vadis?*, a trend that had begun in the 1920s and was clearly evident in 1932's *The Sign of the Cross*. Yet by the 1950s, even the sins of Rome could not guarantee box-office profits, and many productions offered new gimmicks and slants to insure success. The story of *The Robe* (1953) suffered in relationship to the debut of the wide-screen CinemaScope process in which it was filmed. Spectacle was the real story of both versions of *Ben-Hur*, as sea battles and chariot races received more time and attention than specifics about Jesus or his teachings. *King of Kings* (1961) attempted to exploit the youth market by casting teen heartthrob Jeffrey Hunter as Christ; the picture was tarred by critics and failed at the box office. The Italian productions of *Barabbas* (1962) and *Pontius Pilate* (1967) tried

to rejuvenate the subject by telling Christ's story from the viewpoint of their respective title characters, but both films were, in the final analysis, little more than greater and lesser variations on the then-popular sword-and-sandal action epics, with the Gospels and the faithful replacing the Greco-Roman pantheon and its followers.

In 1966, Pier Paolo Pasolini's controversial *The Gospel According to St. Matthew* was released in America, and in almost every way it contrasted sharply with George Stevens's reverent-to-a-fault *The Greatest Story Ever Told*, released the previous year. Pasolini's was an Italian production, filmed predominantly on Italy's rocky coast, and shot on a modest budget with a cast of nonprofessionals. Unlike any such biblical movie previously filmed, it showed a gritty Judea populated by remarkably average-looking people. But its most strik-

THE SIGN OF THE CROSS: A spectacular arena scene.

ing departure from its predecessors was in its portrayal of an all-too-human Christ with a definite message for his followers. Differing from past incarnations, this Jesus displays a far wider range of emotions, giving the man and his message of spiritual redemption an urgency and vitality refreshing in its honesty. *America* magazine echoed this in its review:

> Despite its extreme unpretentiousness, its incompleteness, its deliberate lack of ethnic and topographical authenticity, it does succeed in comforting us with the reality of Christ's life and teaching, not in the comfortable context of the no-longer relevant past, but as a direct and ever-renewing challenge in every age.

Some of the recent attempts to humanize Christ have brought with them a host of new problems. Strongly criticized (sight unseen) by religious groups when it was first televised, the miniseries *Jesus of Nazareth* (1977) initially provoked controversy because of public statements by director Franco Zeffirelli stressing Jesus's humanity over his divinity. These inflammatory comments proved to be false; after it aired the same people who initially villified the project then embraced it as one of the most reverent portrayals of Christ ever filmed.

The most controversial movie adaptation to date of Jesus's life, Martin Scorsese's *The Last Temptation of Christ* (1988), which, unlike *Jesus of Nazareth*, has yet to win mainstream acceptance, presents a darker view of Jesus, showing a disruptive joining of the divine and human, resulting in an almost constant emotional battle being fought within Christ. Scorsese's film is as radical a departure from current portrayals as *The Gospel According to St. Matthew* had been, because it uses that emotional conflict to reinterpret the characters in the Gospels. Jesus's relationships with Judas and Mary Magdalene are established as being much deeper and more complicated than ever previously shown. This, and Satan's final temptation of Jesus on the cross, were the two most daring—and most protested—aspects of the production. Yet, there is nothing in the story that revises or contradicts the New Testament.

Instead, the film makes an attempt to explain realistically the vague backgrounds and motivations of the characters in the Gospels while staying within the framework of those texts. When taken as a whole, the production is a refreshing, if unsettling, look at Jesus and his times. *The Last Temptation of Christ* succeeds by showing Jesus grappling with his dual nature, eventually realizing his greater purpose, and rising to fulfill his destiny on the cross. The film fails to an extent by stopping short and avoiding a literal Resurrection, ending after the Crucifixion in an explosion of impressionistic light open to varied interpretation.

Directorial viewpoint aside, the actor portraying Christ in *any* film is trapped in a maze of dramatic contradictions; he must be believably human, yet also believably divine, gentle yet forceful, charismatic yet humble. Small wonder that many otherwise good actors have fallen short attempting to interpret this complicated, prismatic role, as multilayered and difficult as anything in Shakespeare. The viewer watching any screen portrait of this sort—especially the devout viewer—must remember that films are not Holy Writ; they exist on a different level entirely, designed for the most part with the intent of appealing to—and profiting from—a commercial audience. The teachings of Jesus Christ remain eternal, but just as fifteenth-century artists painted the Crucifixion depicting Roman soldiers attired in contemporary fifteenth century armor, so does modern society's image of Jesus seem to shift and change as society itself changes.

It is not the purpose of *Divine Images* to either instigate or attempt to resolve any theological debate. We make no pretense of writing from a religious point of view. What we have attempted to do is to present a comprehensive examination of motion pictures based on Jesus's life. This book is a sincere attempt to catalogue every significant film depicting either Jesus Christ or individuals and events directly connected to his life. Editorial selectivity naturally leads to the exclusion of some titles. Allegories involving Christ-like figures, such as *The Passing of the Third Floor Back* (both 1917 and 1936 versions), *Destination Unknown*

THE GREATEST STORY EVER TOLD: Max Von Sydow (center).

THE GOSPEL ACCORDING TO ST. MATTHEW: The Last Supper.

THE LAST TEMPTATION OF CHRIST: Willem Dafoe.

(1933), and *Strange Cargo* (1940) are included here, while others that stray farther afield in their treatment and are subject to varied interpretation, like the Sidney Poitier film, *Brother John* (1972), are not. Neither are most documentaries and pseudo-documentaries, such as *The St. Matthew Passion* (1952), *Rembrandt's Christ* (1964), and *Beyond and Back* (1978), unless we feel that such movies contain enough specially-filmed dramatic material to warrant their inclusion. Only the most noteworthy television productions are discussed.

Dramatic films that contain only fleeting glimpses of Jesus, but do not otherwise concern themselves with the subject, are also excluded; among them, *The Birth of a Nation* (1915) and *Sparrows* (1926). Otherwise unrelated films that use brief appearances by Christ or Christ-like figures merely for shock or satirical effect are not examined; this category includes such diverse titles as *L'Age D'Or* (1930), *Gas-s-s-s* (1970), *A Clockwork Orange* (1971), *The Devils* (1971), *Savage Messiah* (1972), *The Trial of Billy Jack* (1974), and *The Visitor* (1980). Sub-professional, amateur productions like *The Sin of Jesus* (1961) and *Multiple Maniacs* (1970) also are excluded. So are animated films such as *The Star of Bethlehem* (both 1921 and 1969 versions) and pornography like *Him* (1974) and *I Saw Jesus Die* (1976).

In addition to these exceptions, most privately financed productions filmed by church and religious organizations have been omitted; it would require a book in itself to document the countless subjects in this category, and the central purpose of *Divine Images* is, after all, to provide an illustrated history of how the mainstream cinema has dealt with the subject of Jesus Christ within the restrictions of a commercial market.

ROY KINNARD AND TIM DAVIS
Chicago, Illinois
April 1992

18

CHAPTER 1

THE EARLY SILENTS

1897–1919

THE PASSION PLAY OF OBERAMMERGAU

1898 Edison

CREDITS

Producers: Richard G. Hollaman, Albert G. Eaves; *Director:* Henry C. Vincent; *Based on the play by* Salmi Morse; *Photography:* William C. Paley. *Length:* 2,100 feet.

CAST

Frank Russell played *Jesus* in a cast that included: Frank Gaylor (*Judas Iscariot*); Fred Strong (*Pontius Pilate*).

COMMENTARY

In the late 1890s, the producers of the earliest motion pictures quickly realized that greater profits could be earned only through the presentation of a more respectable product. With the public tiring of the nickelodeon clips depicting not much more than street scenes and novelty vignettes, desperate film manufacturers turned to novels and stage plays for inspiration, and in the final years of the nineteenth century, the newborn motion picture medium began its first tentative steps toward attaining the status of an art form. The Holy Bible was one of the first dramatic works adapted to the screen, simply because it presented filmmakers with material that was not only popular but dignified.

In the summer of 1897, W. B. Hurd, who represented pioneering French film entrepreneur Auguste Lumiére in America, thought of filming the annual staging of *The Passion Play* (a traditional church pageant depicting the highlights of Christ's life) in Horwitz, Bohemia, after witnessing the folk pageant during a trip to Europe. Hurd presented his idea to Rich G. Hollaman of New York's Eden Musee, where motion pictures were exhibited as novelties along with death masks of celebrities, wax effigies of criminals, and other curiosities. An intrigued Hollaman assured Hurd that he had a deal (for $10,000), and that the agreement would be finalized after Hollaman returned from an upcoming trip. When Hollaman did return, only ten days later, he found that Hurd had impetuously sold the rights to theatrical producers Marc Klaw and Abraham Erlanger, who proceeded to film *The Passion Play* (Klaw & Erlanger, 1897) on location in Europe.

The resulting Klaw-Erlanger documentary footage of the pageant, supervised and photographed by W. W. "Doc" Freeman, was crudely shot and disappointed audiences when it was screened in Philadelphia, but among the spectators were Hollaman and an actor friend, Frank Russell. Although the Klaw-Erlanger film had not been very impressive, Hollaman was still determined to outdo the competition. Hollaman recalled that seventeen years earlier, Salmi Morse, a dramatist from San Francisco, had attempted to establish himself in the New York theatre by staging an ambitious production of *The Passion Play* at the Rialto on Broadway, joining forces with the eminent theatrical producer, Henry G. Abbey. The play was mounted at a cost of $40,000 and was prepared to open during the 1880–81 season when the mayor of New York, wary of delicate religious sensibilities and the attendant political implications, ordered the production shut down. The expensive props and costumes were thrown into storage, along with Morse's scenario. A dispirited failure, Morse died a few years later, and Abbey, gradually losing control of his business interests, passed away on October 17, 1896.

The Morse-Abbey *Passion Play* properties were being held by a costume company owned by Albert G. Eaves (an acquaintance of Hollaman's friend, Frank Russell). When Hollaman proposed that the three of them collaborate on a filmed recreation of *The Passion Play*, which they would shoot on the roof of New York's Grand Central Palace, Eaves agreed. Russell, the first professional actor cast in the role on film, would play Jesus, with Frank Gaylor as Judas Iscariot and Fred Strong as Pontius Pilate. The primitive film was photographed by William C. Paley. An Englishman, Paley had designed and constructed his own movie camera, circumventing the legal scrutiny of the monopolistic Thomas A. Edison Company, which sought total patent control over the manufacture and sale of all motion picture cameras and projectors.

With Salmi Morse's neglected stage scenario dusted off and serving as a makeshift screenplay, filming lurched ahead in December of 1897 before painted backdrops on the Grand Central Palace roof. The nominal director was stage veteran Henry C. Vincent, but, with theatrical technique firmly ingrained in his methods, he simply could not master the entirely different narrative requirements of film or even grasp the fundamentals of motion picture photography. For several reasons, the bumbling Vincent could not be fired, so Frank Russell and William Paley managed to force him out of the production each day by claiming that the available sunlight was too weak for photography, and then going on to direct the film themselves after his departure.

The completed picture, *The Passion Play of Oberammergau*, containing twenty-three separate scenes running a total of nineteen minutes, was first shown at the Eden Musee on January 30, 1898, with spoken narration delivered by Frank Oakes Ross (descriptive title cards had not yet been developed). There were two screenings a day, and, to prevent his being recognized, Frank Russell was barred from attending. Rivals Klaw and Erlanger unsuccessfully attempted to block the exhibition, and may well have been responsible for leaking word to the press that the movie had not been filmed in Oberammergau (the Bavarian town where a famous version of *The Passion Play* was regularly staged), but was only a faked re-creation shot in New York. After a week of highly-praised screenings, the news that the footage had been staged finally broke in the *New York Herald*, but the adverse publicity had little effect, and prints of the popular film were even sold to other exhibitors for $850 a copy. The Edison Company, finally cognizant of the Hollaman-Eaves film, asserted its corporate patent authority and was awarded possession of the negative. The twenty-three original segments were broken up and sold individually to exhibitors in the Edison catalogue (a 35mm fragment of *The Passion Play of Oberammergau* survives today in the George Eastman House archives in Rochester, New York).

Although Hollaman and Eaves had pro-

THE PASSION PLAY OF OBERAMMERGAU: The Crucifixion; Frank Russell (center).

duced their film solely as competition for the Klaw and Erlanger movie, they had, by faking and dramatizing scenes, unwittingly taken one of the first steps toward artistic expression in motion pictures, inspiring contemporary pioneers like Sigmund Lubin to imitate their effort.

FROM THE MANGER TO
THE CROSS

1913 Kalem

CREDITS

Director: Sidney Olcott; *Screenplay:* Sidney Olcott, Gene Gauntier; *Photography:* George K. Hollister; *Set Design:* Dr. Schick. *Length:* 6 reels.

CAST

Robert Henderson-Bland played *Jesus* in a cast that included: Gene Gauntier (*the Virgin Mary*); Jack Clark (*John, the Beloved Disciple*); Robert J. Vignola (*Judas*); Percy Dyer (*Jesus as a Boy*); Alice Hollister (*Mary Magdalene*); Helen Lindroth (*Martha*); J. P. McGowan (*Andrew*); Sydney Baber (*Lazarus*); Sidney Olcott (*Blind Man*).

COMMENTARY

From the Manger to the Cross (subtitled *Jesus of Nazareth*) is in many ways the finest silent movie version of Christ's life. The film derives most of its charm from its unpretentious simplicity. The script, by actress Gene Gauntier (who also plays the Virgin Mary), is a straightforward adaptation of the New Testament, employing quotations from the Gospels as title cards.

Jesus is portrayed, in a subdued and dignified manner, by Robert Henderson-Bland, who exhibits none of the overwrought histrionics commonly associated with silent film acting. Henderson-Bland was so obsessed with the role that he wrote two books docu-

FROM THE MANGER TO THE CROSS: Robert Henderson-Bland as Jesus.

FROM THE MANGER TO THE CROSS: Robert Henderson-Bland.

menting his portrayal, *From the Manger to the Cross* (published in 1922) and *Actor–Soldier–Poet* (published in 1939).

From the Manger to the Cross is a careful dramatization of the highlights of Christ's life much in the fashion of the various Passion Plays, but given more of an emotional charge by Olcott's imaginative direction. As an example, when the Miracle at Cana is shown, the changing of the water into wine is depicted when Henderson-Bland suddenly assumes a dramatic pose and a quick burst of miraculous light flashes across his face. Earlier in the film, when Jesus is shown as a young boy carrying a wood plank near his father's carpentry shop, sunlight angles toward the youth so that the prophetic shadow of a cross appears on the ground.

Although one or two interior sets are cheaply designed, *From the Manger to the Cross* benefits greatly from on-location filming, with real landmarks such as the Great Pyramids

forming impressive backdrops that no studio re-creation of 1913 could have matched. Filmed on a reported budget of $100,000, the picture looks far more expensive than it actually was. The most successful film produced by Kalem, it was kept in circulation for years, and a quarter of a century later, after Kalem had ceased to exist as a production entity, it was reissued (in 1937) with a synchronized music and sound effects track, together with newly-filmed close-ups, which were edited into the original footage.

INTOLERANCE

1916 Wark Releasing Company

CREDITS

Director/Producer/Screenplay: D. W. Griffith; *Photography:* G. W. Bitzer, Karl Brown; *Music Score:* Joseph

FROM THE MANGER TO THE CROSS: Mary and Joseph before the Sphinx in Egypt; filmed on location.

Carl Breil, D. W. Griffith; *Film Editors:* James Smith, Rose Smith; *Set Designer:* Frank "Huck" Wortman; *Property Master:* Ralph DeLacy; *Assistant Directors:* Arthur Berthelon, Allan Dwan, Erich von Stroheim, Christy Cabanne, Tod Browning, Jack Conway, George Nicholls, Lloyd Ingraham. *Length:* 14 reels.

CAST

Howard Gaye played *Jesus* in a cast that included: Lillian Gish (*The Woman Who Rocks the Cradle*); THE MODERN STORY: Mae Marsh (*The Dear One*); Fred Turner (*Her Father*); Robert Harron (*The Boy*); Sam de Grasse (*Arthur Jenkins*); Vera Lewis (*Mary T. Jenkins*); Mary Alden, Pearl Elmore, Lucille Browne, Luray Huntley, Mrs. Arthur Mackley (*The "Uplifters"*); Miriam Cooper (*The Friendless One*); Walter Long (*The Musketeer of the Slums*); Tully Marshall (*A Friend of the Musketeer*); Tom Wilson (*The Kindly Policeman*); Ralph Lewis (*The Governor*); Lloyd Ingraham (*The Judge*); Barney Bernard (*Attorney for the Boy*); Rev. A. W. McClure (*Father Farley*); Max Davidson (*The Kindly Neighbor*); Monte Blue (*A Striker*); Marguerite Marsh (*A Debutante Guest at the Ball*); Jennie Lee (*Woman at Jenkins Employees' Dance*); Tod Browning (*Owner of the Racing Car*); Edward Dillon (*Chief Detective*); Clyde Hopkins (*Jenkins's Secretary*); William Brown (*The Warden*), Alberta Lee (*Wife of the Kindly Neighbor*); THE JUDEAN STORY: Lillian Langdon (*Mary, the Mother*); Olga Grey (*Mary Magdalene*); Gunther von Ritzau, Erich von Stroheim (*Pharisees*); Bessie Love (*The Bride of Cana*); George Walsh (*The Bridegroom*); THE FRENCH STORY: Margery Wilson (*Brown Eyes*); Eugene Pallette (*Prosper Latour*); Spottiswoode Aitken (*Brown Eyes's Father*); Ruth Handforth (*Brown Eyes's Mother*); A. D. Sears (*The Mercenary*); Frank Bennett (*Charles IX*); Maxfield Stanley (*Mons. La France, Duc d'Anjou*); Josephine Crowell (*Catherine de Medici*); Constance Talmadge (*Marguerite de Valois*); W. E. Lawrence (*Henry of Navarre*); Joseph Henabery (*Adm. Coligny*); Morris Levy (*Duc de Guise*); Howard Gaye (*Cardinal Lorraine*); Louis Romaine (*A Catholic Priest*); THE BABYLONIAN STORY: Constance Talmadge (*The Mountain Girl*); Elmer Clifton (*The Rapsode*); Alfred Paget (*Belshazzar*); Seena Owen (*Attarea, the Princess Beloved*); Carl Stockdale (*King Nabonidus*); Tully Marshall (*High

INTOLERANCE: The huge Babylonian set.

INTOLERANCE: The Wedding at Cana; Howard Gaye (left), with Bessie Love and George Walsh (right) as the bride and groom.

Priest of Bel); George Siegmann (Cyrus, the Persian); Elmo Lincoln (The Mighty Man of Valor); George Fawcett (A Babylonian Judge); Kate Bruce (A Babylonian Mother); Ruth St. Denis (Solo Dancer); Loyola O'Connor (Attarea's Slave); James Curley (The Charioteer of Cyrus); Howard Scott (A Babylonian Dandy); Alma Rubens, Ruth Darling, Margaret Mooney (Girls of the Marriage Market); Mildred Harris, Pauline Starke (Favorites of the Harem); Winifred Westover (The Favorite of Egibi); Grace Wilson (First Dancer of Tammuz); Lotta Clifton (Second Dancer of Tammuz); Ah Singh (First Priest of Nergel); Ranji Singh (Second Priest of Nergel); Ed Burns (Second Charioteer of the Priest of Bel); Martin Landry (Auctioneer); Wallace Reid (A Boy Killed in the Fighting); Charles Eagle Eye (Barbarian Chieftain); Charles Van Courtlandt (Gobyras, Lieutenant of Cyrus); Jack Cosgrove (Chief Eunuch).

COMMENTARY

Conceived by pioneering film director D. W. Griffith as an encore to his previous milestone effort, The Birth of a Nation (1915), Intolerance has been aptly described as the cinema's only "film fugue." Presenting four separate narratives set in disparate historical periods (Babylonian, Judean, French Revolutionary, and Modern), and linked only by the symbolic shot of a rocking temporal cradle, Griffith sought to demonstrate the innate goodness of humanity, and to show how, despite the overpowering deceit and treachery repeatedly arrayed in opposition to those qualities, peace and love must and will ultimately triumph. Intolerance is the product of a man who not only believed so wholeheartedly in the then-new medium of

26

film that he was willing to risk (and eventually lose) his personal fortune in order to make it, but also had a basic faith in his fellow men. As such, it is one of the most audacious films ever made, and one of the very few motion pictures that can be legitimately described as a work of art. When it is seen in the form of a good print, appropriately color-tinted, and projected at the correct speed, *Intolerance* still impresses today.

A large portion of Griffith's then-opulent budget of $1.9 million was absorbed by the massive Babylonian set, erected in Los Angeles. Lacking the technical finesse of convincing miniatures and optical mattes (procedures not yet fully developed by the fledgling industry), this mammoth set had to be built in full scale out of necessity. Wisely, Griffith never allowed the immense physical proportions of the Babylonian story to overwhelm the human drama, and some of the performances are quite good, particularly that of Constance Talmadge as The Mountain Girl.

The Judean scenes, although brief, are (like the rest of the film) shot with such graceful beauty that they leave more of a lasting impression than many a later biblical epic entirely devoted to the subject. A subdued Howard Gaye plays Jesus in scenes depicting the Miracle at Cana and the Crucifixion. Although Gaye's sequences occupy only a small portion of the total running time, his impressive portrayal ranks as one of the most successful dramatizations of Christ on film, and the early shot of Gaye standing near a flock of doves is one of the loveliest scenes in the silent cinema. The Miracle at Cana is beautifully filmed, with a symbolic double-exposed crucifix obscuring Gaye as the water is changed to wine. Comparing this scene with the similar one in director Sidney Olcott's earlier *From the Manger to the Cross*, that version (as previously described) is dramatic and effective, but Griffith's handling of the same material is far more poetic and memorable. According to contemporary reports, Griffith encountered censorship difficulties when the B'nai B'rith objected to scenes he had filmed showing the Jewish leaders crucifying Jesus; the director acquiesced to the pressure and burned the negative already shot, refilming the scenes with Roman soldiers substituted.

Although *Intolerance* was certainly a commercial failure, with many in its contemporary audience confused and intimidated by the difficult, crosscutting narrative, the film endures as a unique touchstone work of the silent era, its occasional crudeness and naïveté far outshone by its undeniable artistry.

REVIEWS

. . . For in spite of its utter incoherence, the questionable taste of some of its scenes and the cheap banalities into which it sometimes lapses, *Intolerance* is an interesting and unusual picture.

New York Times

It is a full three-hours' entertainment, comprising a prolog and two acts and its undoubted success will be due to the magnificence of the investiture, which reflects much credit to the wizard director, for it required no small amount of genuine art to consistently blend actors, horses, monkeys, geese, doves, acrobats, and ballet into a composite presentation of a film classic . . . A detailed analysis would occupy pages and then fall short. Mr. Griffith has a film that goes a step beyond his contemporaries.

Variety

MORE EARLY SILENTS

The earliest biblical films were brief, simple recordings of *The Passion Play*, and the first two of these emanated from France in 1897. Both were titled simply *The Passion*, the first a five-minute short released by Lear, and the second released by Lumiére.

American filmmaker Sigmund Lubin's *The Passion Play* (Lubin, 1898), crudely shot in Philadelphia, was followed by other early French efforts: *The Passion* (Gaum, 1898) and *Christ Walking on the Water* (Méliès, 1899), filmed by the great fantasist Georges Méliès.

A one-reel version of the traditional pageant, *The Passion Play*, containing ten scenes, was directed by Luigi Topi in Italy in 1900.

Soldiers of the Cross (1900) was a unique multimedia Australian production made by the Salvation Army, directed by Joseph Perry and written by Perry in collaboration with Herbert Booth. Perry had been in charge of producing lantern slides on biblical and social topics for the Melbourne Salvation Army; Booth (son of the Salvation Army's founder, General William Booth) recognized the potential value of Perry's work and expanded the activities of Perry's department to include motion picture production. After filming numerous religious short subjects, Perry and Booth concocted *Soldiers of the Cross*, a marathon 135-minute conglomeration of their short films (some depicting Jesus Christ), slides, music, and live narration.

Georges Méliès filmed *The Wandering Jew* (Star, 1904) in France. Based on the novel by Eugene Sue and refilmed several times, this was the story of a Jerusalem merchant who was

INTOLERANCE: Jesus bears his cross to Calvary.

condemned to live through eternity after refusing Christ a moment's rest near his shop as Jesus bore the cross to Calvary.

The Life and Passion of Jesus Christ (Pathé, 1905) was a two-reel French Passion Play directed by Ferdinand Zecca and Lucien Nonget. This was followed by another French two-reeler, *The Life of Christ* (Gaum, 1906), directed by Alice Guy, Victor Jasset, and George Hatot.

One of the most popular books ever written, and a perennial turn-of-the-century stage attraction as well, General Lew Wallace's 1880 novel *Ben-Hur* was the story of a disgraced Jewish noble (the title hero) in Jerusalem who is sold into slavery (with his mother and sister condemned to a leper colony) when he is betrayed by his friend Messala, a Roman centurion. Escaping his fate as a galley slave after a sea battle, Ben-Hur saves the life of the ship's captain, and after being granted his freedom, earns notoriety as a charioteer, ultimately defeating Messala in a fatal chariot race. The tale is punctuated throughout with fleeting appearances by Jesus Christ, who eventually cures Ben-Hur's leprous mother and sister.

The first version of *Ben-Hur*, released by Kalem in 1907, is all but forgotten today, and its obscurity is understandable. Directed by Sidney Olcott and Frank Oakes Ross (who had delivered the spoken narration for *The Passion Play of Oberammergau* at the Eden Musee), the spare one-reel film is only a skeletal version of the novel, offering a few tepid shots of a chariot race intercut with a couple of interiors. The genius of Wallace's novel—scenes with Jesus Christ running parallel to and at times interwoven with the hero's narrative, thus imparting a more immediate human dimension to the religious aspects of the story—would not receive adequate treatment until the spectacular MGM version of 1925. The 1907 *Ben-Hur*, forgettable as it was, did establish an unintended precedent of sorts. The producers had neglected to formally purchase the screen rights to Wallace's novel, and after four years in litigation, Kalem was found to be in violation of copyright laws and was ordered to pay $25,000 in damages. The case firmly established the legal concept of motion picture rights in the adaptation of literary and theatrical properties. Director Sidney Olcott later atoned for his *Ben-Hur* misfire with *From the Manger to the Cross*.

The Life of Jesus (Pathé, 1907) was another French Passion Play short, running a mere five minutes. *The Life of Christ* (1907) was one of the first American versions of *The Passion Play*; this was followed by *Jerusalem in the Time of Christ* (Kalem, 1908), a pseudo-documentary containing a few re-created scenes of Jesus's life.

The first screen version of Oscar Wilde's 1893 play *Salomé*, about the stepdaughter of King Herod who dances to claim John the Baptist's head, was released by Vitagraph on August 29, 1908. A one-reeler, *Salomé* starred Florence Lawrence (in the title role) and Maurice Costello.

The Star of Bethlehem (Edison, 1908) was a ten-minute pageant in eight scenes depicting the Nativity.

The Life and Passion of Jesus Christ (Pathé, 1908) a three-reel French import, featured M. Normand as Jesus, Mme. Moreau as the Virgin Mary, M. Moreau as Joseph, and M. Jacquinett as Judas. Le Petit Briand played Jesus as a boy. This film was a Passion Play staged in the usual tableau form. Inevitably, for a pre-1910 movie, this primitive effort is rather stodgy when viewed today, with unimaginative set design and curiously gauche performers. There are a few crude attempts at special effects, but these are done without the wit and charm of Méliès. Six years later, in 1914, the picture was re-edited, expanded with new footage, enhanced with (uneven) color tinting applied by hand one frame at a time, and released under the title *The Life of Our Saviour*. The reworked picture was reviewed in April 1914 by *Variety*, whose critic was apparently unaware he was watching a film that was partially several years old:

No matter what this person or that person is going to say, the picture leaves a lasting impression that will never be erased. It is going to hand the exhibitor a thrill and make him knit his eyebrows a few times when he shows this picture on the same screen where a few weeks or months before he had some cheap, unhealthy "vice" film.

Still another reedited version appeared in 1921 under the title *Behold the Man!*, in which the colorized 1908 footage was used as biblical counterpoint to a modern (newly-shot) framing story in black and white. As before, the critic for *Variety* did not comment on the age of the vintage 1908 footage, which must have been glaringly obvious by this time. The January 1921 review noted:

> It may be said that this is a possibly interesting but unexceptional photoplay. It is doubtful in any event whether any screen version of the episodic career of Christ, in the strict orthodox sense, can be made interesting to the vast majority of picture-goers.

The new footage in *Behold the Man!* was directed by Spencer Gordon Bennet, later a prolific director of serials at Columbia Pictures in the sound era.

The Birth of Jesus (Pathé, 1909) was another French import, depicting the Nativity in hand-tinted color. Also from France came *The Kiss of Judas* (Film d'Art, 1909), a one-reeler starring M. Lambert and M. Sully, which portrayed The Last Supper and Jesus's betrayal by Judas. *The Passion Play* (Gaumont, 1909) was a British version of the pageant, running two reels and released in color. *Herod and the Newborn King* (Gaumont, 1910), from France, told the story of Joseph and Mary's flight into Egypt to escape King Herod's death warrant against the Savior.

One 1910 production exists today only in the form of unedited shots that were probably filmed for the George Kleine production, *The Life and Passion of Christ*. A 16mm print of the unedited footage, depicting various events in Jesus's life, is on file in the Library of Congress.

Resurrection of Lazarus (Eclair, 1910) was a French one-reeler dramatizing the title event. Other French productions of the period were *Jesus* (1911), starring Jacques Guilhene; *The Miracle* (Eclipse, 1911), a one-reeler that showed Jesus restoring life to the murdered infant prince of a Ruritanian kingdom; and *The Mysterious Stranger* (Eclipse, 1911), a contemporary one-reel drama in which Jesus appears in modern times and raises the dead, in this case, a farmer's daughter who had been struck by lightning. *Though Your Sins Be as Scarlet*, released by Vitagraph on April 22, 1911, featured Charles Kent as Jesus and Julia Swayne Gordon as Mary Magdalene.

The Illumination, a one-reel production released by Vitagraph on August 5, 1912, was an imaginative drama showing the effect of Jesus's influence on two people: Joseph, a young Jew, and Maximus, a Roman centurion. Although Jesus is never seen as an actual figure, his presence is indicated by a light falling on the characters' faces. *The Pilgrim* (Ambrosio, 1912) was an Italian effort directed by Mario Casserini; an existing publicity photo shows Jesus being crowned with thorns by a Roman soldier. *Satan*, also known as *Satan, or the Drama of Humanity*, was another 1912 Italian production released by Ambrosio. Directed by Luigi Maggi, the screenplay by Guido Volente was based on the poems *Paradise Lost* by John Milton and *The Messiah* by Fredrich Klopstock. This seven-reel drama, starring Maria Bonnard, Rina Alby, Mary Cleo Tarlarina, and Antonio Grisanti, foreshadowed the basic concept of D. W. Griffith's *Intolerance* by examining Satan's influence on humanity through the ages; included was a biblical sequence depicting Christ's life. *Saved by Divine Providence* (Pathé, 1912) was a modern story with Jesus appearing to lead a mother to her lost son. *The Star of Bethlehem*, a three-reeler released by Thanhouser on Christmas Eve 1912, was written and directed by Theodore Marston, and featured William Russell, Florence LaBadie, Harry Benham, James Cruze, and Marguerite Snow. The film presented another version of the Nativity; a tattered print still exists in the Library of Congress.

The Carpenter, a one-reeler released by Vitagraph on July 15, 1913, was a Civil War drama with a twist; Jesus Christ appears during the War Between the States as a stranger who reunites the opposing members of a family thrown into turmoil by the conflict. Directed by Wilfred North from a screenplay by Marguerite Bertsch, the film starred Earle Williams, Lillian Walker, and Charles Kent. *The Crimson Cross* (Eclair, 1913) was a French three-reeler examining the mysteries of the Rosary within the framework of a story set in Puritan New England; the bulk of the film's concluding two reels was a biblical flashback containing a twenty-scene outline of Jesus's life. *The Wandering Jew* (Roma, 1913) was a five-reel Italian adaptation of the Eugene Sue novel. Also from Italy came *Salomé* (European Feature Films, 1913), featuring a scantily-clad Suzanne de Laarboy as the dancer in King Herod's court. In its review, Variety found the thirty-seven-minute production disappointingly tame: "While the whole thing is most artistically done, there is nothing in the reels to create sufficient excitement to call out the police—or anybody else."

Another more impressive Italian import was *Quo Vadis?* (Cines-Kleine, 1913), based on the novel by Henryk Sienkiewicz that told of Peter leaving Rome because of the persecution suffered by Christians, only to return when he is confronted by a vision of Christ. Peter asks Jesus, "Quo Vadis?" Translated from Latin, it means "Where are you going?" to which Jesus replies, "I go to Rome, to be crucified again." The film segues into a love triangle involving Vinicius (Amletto Novelli), a Roman soldier, Lygia (Lea Gunghi), the adopted daughter of a Roman general, and Poppaea (Amelia Cattaneo), the Emperor Nero's wife. The story culminates in Nero's burning of Rome and the mass murder of Christians in the Circus Maximus arena, with Vinicius and Lygia surviving at the fadeout.

There had been a crude, one-reel French version of *Quo Vadis?*, directed by Ferdinand Zecca for Pathé in 1902, and another short Pathé version in 1908, but this 1913 film was the first major screen adaptation of the novel. An eight-reel epic directed by Enrico Guazzoni, it was a triumph of art direction and set design as well as artfully composed visuals; so spectacular was the film that American movies of the day seemed inadequate by comparison. When the picture was imported by distributor George Kleine, it played long engagements at legitimate theaters, commanding top ticket prices. The longest film screened in America until that time, it profoundly influenced emerging directors like D. W. Griffith and Cecil B. DeMille. Its tremendous success was instrumental in popularizing the feature-length film.

The Three Wise Men, released by Selig on February 1, 1913, was a fantasy in which amoral Broadway rake Sidney Roger (Thomas Santschi) is transported in a dream sequence to a desert, where he encounters the Three Wise Men, who lead him to the birthplace of Jesus Christ (Frederick W. Huntley). Denied access to the stable because of his sins, Roger suddenly awakens from his traumatic dream and embarks on a repentant new life. The one-reel drama was directed by Colin Campbell from a screenplay by Anthony McGuire. *A Daughter of the Hills*, released on December 27, 1913, by Famous Players, was a three-reeler starring Laura Sawyer and House Peters, Sr. Directed by J. Searle Dawley from his own screenplay, the story involved St. Peter's conversion of a Roman gladiator to Christianity.

Mary Magdalene, released by Kennedy films in February 1914, focused on the courtesan who was reformed by Jesus. Its free-wheeling screenplay all but ignored the Scriptures, postulating a ludicrous soap opera romantic triangle involving Mary, Jesus, and a Roman noble. *The Last Supper*, released by the American Film Manufacturing Co. on April 11, 1914, recounted the title event, with Sydney Ayres playing Jesus. This two-reel drama was directed and written by Lorimer Johnstone. *The Birth of Our Saviour*, a December 12, 1914, release from Edison, was a one-reeler depicting the Nativity and the Flight into Egypt. Directed by Charles Brabin from a screenplay by DeWitt L. Pelton, the film starred Carlton King as Joseph and Gertrude McCoy as the Virgin Mary. Another Italian import, *The Triumph of an Emperor* (Savoia, 1914), offered an account of the Emperor Constantine (Arturo Garzes) liberating Christianity in the fourth century A.D., with an advising vision of Jesus Christ materializing at one point.

Business Is Business, released by Universal on September 13, 1915, was a morality play in which a ruthless industrialist (Nat C. Goodwin) ultimately loses everything in his pursuit of wealth, envisioning Jesus (Hobart Bosworth) at the Last Supper as he dies. The six-reel drama was directed by Otis Turner from a screenplay by F. McGrew Willis, based on the play *Les Affaires Sont Les Affaires* by

Octave Mirabeau.

Pioneering film mogul Thomas H. Ince's ten-reel production of *Civilization* was released on April 17, 1916. Budgeted at $100,000 (although inflated publicity at the time claimed $1 million), this allegorical pacifist tale of war erupting between two mythical kingdoms, with a ghostly, transparent Christ (George Fisher) extolling peace, was highly touted at the time. Seen today, though, the film does not hold up very well; comparisons to Griffith's *Intolerance*, released later the same year, are inevitable, and *Civilization* falls short on almost every level. Ince was simply not in the same directorial league as Griffith, and his cast, led by Howard Hickman and Enid Markey, is vastly inferior to Griffith's. The fictional, pseudo-Germanic setting is also an impediment, only distancing and weakening what should have been visceral drama with personal emotional impact for the viewer. Although sincere and financially successful, *Civilization* was a flawed picture receiving mixed reviews, and the film's demand for peace was ignored after the beginning of World War I. With pacifism on the decline as war hysteria gripped the nation, Ince proved himself somewhat opportunistic in hurriedly reediting *Civilization*, inserting patriotic shots of the American flag, Woodrow Wilson's congressional speech, and rewritten, jingoistic title cards. In England, the picture was even refurbished to include military recruiting scenes and given the title *What Every True Briton Is Fighting For*. In 1931, *Civilization* was rereleased in a shortened six-reel version, with synchronized music and color tinting.

Light at Dusk, a July 31, 1916, Lubin release, was a moralistic tale about a social-climbing Russian peasant (Orrin Johnson), consumed by greed, who achieves success in America as a financial tycoon, exploiting the workers in his factory. When his wife dies, he sees a vision of Jesus Christ and reforms. The six-reel film was directed by Edgar Lewis from a screenplay by Anthony P. Kelly.

The Warfare of the Flesh, released in May 1917, by Edward Warren Productions, was a seven-reel allegory examining the struggle between good and evil from the Garden of Eden through the time of Christ and on to the present day as a virtuous woman (Charlotte Ives) is nearly forced to compromise her morals in order to save her dying husband. The film, the first effort of Edward Warren Productions, was directed by Warren from a screenplay he cowrote with Lawrence Marston. The picture was filmed at the Brenon Studios and on location in Florida and North Carolina. *The Warfare of the Flesh* was also distributed under the alternate titles *Souls Redeemed* and *Transgressors*.

Christus (Cines, 1917), an Italian production, was directed on location in Europe in 1915 by Count Giulio Antamoro and starred Giovanni Pasquali as Jesus. The six-reel film was based on the poem of the same title by Fausto Salvatori, and in presenting the traditional highlights of Christ's life, drew visual inspiration from religious paintings by Da Vinci, Donatello, Rembrandt, Mantegna, and others. The American premiere boasted an orchestral accompaniment of classical music performed by an assembly of musicians from the Philharmonic Symphony, the Boston Symphony, and the Metropolitan Opera.

The Passing of the Third Floor Back (Ideal, 1917) was a British feature directed by Herbert Brenon, and based on Jerome K. Jerome's allegorical play about a mysterious stranger (presumed to be Jesus Christ) who lodges at a boarding house and influences the lives of those around him. The play had been a theatrical success for lead James Forbes-Robertson, who was also featured in this six-reel film version. Similar in basic theme to the much later MGM sound picture *Strange Cargo* (1940), *The Passing of the Third Floor Back* was distributed in the United States by First National in 1918.

An unreleased Thomas Edison film of 1917, production #2454, which was apparently to have been titled *Crossing the Bar* (probably after the poem of the same title by Alfred Lord Tennyson), contained a scene of Jesus Christ appearing before a fisherman in a sailboat. A 16mm print of the unedited footage survives in the Library of Congress.

Morok (Hesperia, 1918), also known as *Morok, the Standard Bearer of the Jewish People*, was another Italian version of Eugene Sue's novel *The Wandering Jew*. *The Unbeliever*, released by Edison on February 9, 1918, was based on the novelette *The Three Things* by Mary Raymond Shipman Andrews, and dealt with the callous scion (Raymond McKee) of a wealthy New York family, who enlists in the Marine Corps during World War I, gradually losing his class and racial prejudices and reforming for good after seeing a vision of Christ when he is wounded in combat. The seven-reel film was produced with the cooperation of the Marine Corps, and Erich von Stroheim, soon to emerge as a prestigious director at Universal, appeared as a brutal German officer.

Restitution, released on May 12, 1918, is a genuine oddity. Directed by and starring Howard Gaye, who reprises his portrayal of Jesus from *Intolerance*, the film depicts man's struggle against Satan through the ages, culminating in modern times as Satan reappears to form an unholy alliance with Kaiser Wilhelm, only to be eventually defeated by Christ. A substantial production, *Restitution* was the first effort of the newly-formed Mena Film Co., and was in production for six months, using over fifty sets. The release prints were to have been colored. In the late 1920s, the film was reissued by Ideal Pictures under the title *The Conquering Christ*. Although the original length of *Restitution* was reportedly nine to twelve reels, the 16mm print on file at the American Film Institute, bearing the title *The Conquering Christ*, is considerably shorter.

Salomé, released by Fox in October 1918, starred Hollywood femme fatale Theda Bara in a seven-reel version of the familiar tale, although this time, according to the *New York Times* in its review, ". . . The story of Salomé as told by Josephus, and not that familiar from the Bible, was used as the basis of the film. . ." Bara's flimsy attire, daring for the period, caused a furor among religious groups. The film was directed by J. Gordon Edwards, from a screenplay by Adrian Johnson. A later Metro production of 1920, *A Modern Salomé*, contained sequences based on the Salomé story.

What Shall We Do With Him? released by the World Film Corp. on February 10, 1919, was a five-reel World War I fantasy in which, after presenting opening accounts of Genesis and Jesus's life, the suggestion was made that Kaiser Wilhelm is the Antichrist. Trade articles implied that the film contained documentary footage of the war. *What Shall We Do With Him?* was originally announced for distribution (in 1918) under the title *Unconditional Surrender*. The film was directed by Harry Revier from a screenplay by Hugh C. Weir and Roy Summerville.

Thou Shalt Not, released by Fox on March 23, 1919, was a social drama starring Evelyn Nesbitt (a key figure in the infamous real-life 1906 Thaw–White murder trial) as Ruth, a small-town New England girl who, when abandoned by her lover, is ostracized. Although the local minister (Crawford Kent), secretly in love with her, preaches tolerance by relating how Christ forgave Mary Magdalene, Ruth is still not accepted. Disgusted with the hypocrites in his congregation, the minister leaves town with Ruth to begin a new life together. This six-reel film was directed and written by Charles J. Brabin.

The Eternal Light, released in May 1919 by the Catholic Art Association, was a church production dramatizing the life of Christ, edited by Otto E. Goebel and Conde B. Pallen. The film was shown at a temple in Boston, but was barred from further screenings by the State Police chief because of the acts of violence included in the story. No further information about this eight-reel film is available.

The Eternal Magdalene, released by Goldwyn on April 20, 1919, was a five-reel dramatic allegory in which a respected citizen, Elijah Bradshaw (Charles Dalton), and a preacher (Vernon Steele) lead an evangelical drive to eradicate prostitution in their town. When Bradshaw finds that his own daughter (Margaret Marsh) is romantically involved with his secretary (Donald Gallaher), he drives her from his home. In a subsequent dream sequence, Bradshaw is confronted by Mary Magdalene (Maxine Elliott), who cites the tolerance of Jesus Christ and in a vision shows

SALOMÉ (1918): Theda Bara in the title role.

Bradshaw the consequences of his overzealous actions on the lives of his daughter and others. Awakening in horror, Bradshaw reforms. Directed by Arthur Hopkins from a script based on the stage play by Robert H. McLaughlin (which also featured Maxine Elliott), *The Eternal Magdalene* was actually filmed in 1917, but due to censorship difficulties in Chicago and Philadelphia, it was not released until 1919.

The Woman of Lies, released by the World Film Corp. on October 13, 1919, was a drama about a young woman (Olive Sherman) with a shady past who is engaged to a newspaperman (Earl Metcalfe). The journalist's mother learns of the girl's reputation and forbids the marriage, but she finally relents after seeing a vision of Jesus Christ and Mary Magdalene. The five-reel picture was directed by Gilbert Hamilton from a screenplay by J. Clarkson Miller and Forrest Halsey.

THE KING OF KINGS (1927): H. B. Warner.

CHAPTER 2

THE NINETEEN TWENTIES

BEN-HUR

1925 Metro-Goldwyn-Mayer

CREDITS

Director: Fred Niblo; *Producers:* Louis B. Mayer, Samuel Goldwyn, Irving Thalberg; *Screenplay:* Bess Meredyth, Carey Wilson, *adaptation by* June Mathis (*based on the novel by* Lew Wallace); *Photography (Technicolor sequences)*: Rene Guissart, Percy Hilburn, Karl Struss, Clyde De Vinna, E. Burton Steele, George Meehan; *Special Effects Photography:* Paul Eagler; *Music Score:* William Axt, David Mendoza; *Sets:* Cedric Gibbons, Horace Jackson, Arnold Gillespie; *Titles:* Katherine Hilliker, H. H. Caldwell; *Additional Direction (Nativity Sequence):* Ferdinand P. Earle; *2nd Unit Director:* B. Reaves Eason; *Art Effects:* Ferdinand P. Earle; *Film Editors:* Lloyd Nosler, Basil Wrangell, William Holmes, Harry Reynolds, Ben Lewis; *Assistant Director:* Charles Stallings; *Production Manager:* Harry Edington; *Production Assistants:* Silas Clegg, Alfred Raboch, William Wyler; *Wardrobe:* Hermann J. Kaufmann; *Matte Photography:* Frank D. Williams. *Length:* 12 reels (11,693 feet).

CAST

Ramon Novarro (*Ben-Hur*); Francis X. Bushman (*Messala*); May McAvoy (*Esther*); Betty Bronson (*Mary*); Claire McDowell (*Princess of Hur*); Katherine Key (*Tirzah*); Carmel Myers (*Iras*); Nigel De Brulier (*Simonides*); Mitchell Lewis (*Sheik Ilderman*); Leo White (*Sanballat*); Frank Currier (*Arrius*); Charles Belcher (*Balthasar*); Dale Fuller (*Amrah*); Winter Hall (*Joseph*).

COMMENTARY

Produced at a cost of nearly $4 million, this second film version of *Ben-Hur* was a faithful and satisfying adaptation of the Lew Wallace novel. It was, and remains, a sincere, heartfelt, and beautifully produced epic. The picture cannot be faulted in terms of spectacle; the massive full-scale sea battles and the chariot race are still impressive today, and in terms of sheer opulence—massive sets, special effects, stuntwork, the incredible size of the cast—*Ben-Hur* is one of the outstanding popular entertainments of the silent era.

The opening Nativity sequence, exquisitely filmed in two-strip Technicolor and directed by Ferdinand P. Earle (after Fred Niblo refused to be associated with the scenes), features the best performance in the film, a serene Betty Bronson as the Virgin Mary, while the remaining bulk of the narrative deftly outlines the conflict between Ben-Hur (Ramon Novarro) and Messala (Francis X. Bushman), climaxing in the famous chariot race. There are certainly flaws: Ben-Hur's various trials and tribulations are, as in the 1959 remake, interspersed with occasional scenes depicting Christ, the shots angled so that the unbilled actor playing Jesus is always offscreen, either gesturing with one arm extended into the frame or posing with his back to the camera. Although this technique is intended to impart reverence, it becomes an exasperating contrivance through repetition, and is even, regrettably, unintentionally comical at times.

Earlier filmmakers did not hesitate to show Christ onscreen in one- and two-reelers, the reticence seen in *Ben-Hur* only developed as film budgets increased and cautious producers grew more wary of offending audiences. In many ways better than the 1959 Charlton Heston remake, this *Ben-Hur* still falls short of D. W. Griffith's much earlier *Intolerance* and, for all its slickness, lacks the textural depth that made the Griffith film a true work of art. In spite of its quality, *Ben-Hur* seemed dated when it was recut and reissued six years later, in 1931, with a synchronized music score and sound-effects track. William Wyler, then an assistant director on the chariot race scene, later directed the Charlton Heston remake.

REVIEWS

There will be no further reason for a future production of *Ben-Hur* for the screen, unless there is some tremendous change in the art of visualization of the dramatic that is as yet unrealized . . . the greatest achievement that has been accomplished on the screen for not only the screen itself, but for all motion picture-dom.

Variety

It is an excellent piece of camera work and a film that is unequaled in the number of extras employed. Moreover, the story is told so well that its scenes are never tedious, and one is apt

BEN-HUR (1925): The chariot race between Messala (Francis X. Bushman, left) and Ben-Hur (Ramon Novarro).

BEN-HUR (1925): Betty Bronson as the Virgin Mary.

to overlook most of the occasionally poor work of the players through the interest aroused by the general effect of the master sequences.

New York Times

THE KING OF KINGS

1927 Producers Distributing Corporation (PDC)

CREDITS

Director/Producer: Cecil B. DeMille; *Screenplay:* Jeannie MacPherson; *Photography (Technicolor sequences):*

Peverell Marley, Fred Westerberg, Jacob A. Badaraco; *Film Editors:* Anne Bauchens, Harold McLernon, Clifford Howard; *Art Directors:* Mitchell Leisen, Anton Grot; *Costumes:* Earl Luick, Gwen Wakeling; *Makeup:* Fred C. Ryle; *Technical Engineers:* Paul Sprunck, Norman Osunn; *Assistant Directors:* William J. Cowen, Roy Burns, Frank Urson; *Research:* Elizabeth McGaffee. Length: 14 reels (13,500 feet).

CAST

H. B. Warner played *Jesus* in a cast that included: Dorothy Cumming (*Mary the Mother*); Ernest Torrence (*Peter*); Joseph Schildkraut (*Judas*); James Neill (*James*); Joseph Striker (*John*); Robert Edeson (*Matthew*); Sidney D'Albrook (*Thomas*); David Imboden (*Andrew*); Charles Belcher (*Philip*); Clayton Packard (*Bartholomew*); Robert Ellsworth (*Simon*); Charles Requa (*James, the Less*); John T. Prince (*Thaddeus*); Jacqueline Logan (*Mary Magdalene*); Rudolph Schildkraut (*Caiaphas, High Priest of Israel*); Sam De Grasse (*The Pharisee*); Casson Ferguson (*The Scribe*); Victor Varconi (*Pontius Pilate, Governor of Judea*); Majel Coleman (*Peculla, Wife of Pilate*); Montagu Love (*The Roman Centurion*); William Boyd (*Simon of Cyrene*); M. Moore (*Mark*); Theodore Kosloff (*Malchus, Captain of the High Priest's Guard*); George Siegmann (*Barabbas*); Julia Faye (*Martha*); Josephine Norman (*Mary of Bethany*); Kenneth Thomson (*Lazarus*); Alan Brooks (*Satan*); Viola Louie (*The Woman Taken in Adultery*); Muriel McCormack (*The Blind Girl*); Clarence Burton (*Dysmas, the Repentant Thief*); James Mason (*Gestas, the Unrepentant Thief*); May Robson (*Mother of Gestas*); Dot Farley (*Maid Servant of Caiaphas*); Hector Samo (*The Galilean Carpenter*); Leon Holmes (*The Imbecile Boy*); Jack Padgen (*Captain of the Roman Guard*); Robert St. Angelo, Redman Finely, James Dime, Richard Alexander, Budd Fine, William De Boar, Robert McKee, Tom London, Edward Schaeffer, Peter Norris, Dick Richards (*Soldiers of Rome*); James Farley (*An Executioner*); Otto Lederer (*Eber, a Pharisee*); Bryant Washburn (*A Young Roman*); Lionel Belmore (*A Roman Noble*); Monte Collins (*A Rich Judean*); Luca Flamma (*A Gallant of Galilee*); Sojin (*A Prince of Persia*); Andre Cheron (*A Wealthy Merchant*); William Costello (*A Babylonian Noble*); Sally Rand (*Slave to Mary Magdalene*); Noble Johnson (*A Charioteer*); WITH Jere Austin, W. Azenberg, Fred Becker, Baldy Belmont, Ed Brady, Joe Bonomo, George Calliga, Fred Cavens, Colin Chase, Charles Clary, Denis D'Auburn, Victor de Linsky, Malcolm Denny, David Dunbar, Jack Fife, Sidney Franklin, Kurt

Furberg, Bert Hadley, Edwin Heam, Stanton Heck, Fred Huntley, Brandon Hurst, Otto Kottka, Edward Lackey, Theodore Lorch, Bertram Marburgh, James Marcus, George F. Marion, Earl Metcalf, Max Montor, Louis Natheaux, Richard Neill, Robert Ober, A. Palasthy, Louis Payne, Edward Piel, Albert Priscoe, Herbert Pryor, Warren Rodgers, Charles Sellon, Tom Shirley, Walter Shumway, Bernard Siegel, Phil Sleeman, Charles Stevens, Carl Stockdale, William Strauss, Mark Strong, Josef Swickard, Wilbert Wadleigh, Fred Walker, Will Walling, Paul Weigel, Charles West, Emily Barrye, Elaine Bennett, Lucille Brown, Kathleen Chambers, Edna Mae Cooper, Josephine Crowell, Frances Dale, Milla Davenport, Anna De Linsky, Lillian Elliott, Anielka Elter, Evelyn Francisco, Margaret Francisco, Dale Fuller, Natalie Galitzen, Inez Gomez, Edna Gordon, Julia Swayne Gordon, Winifred Greenwood, Eulalie Jensen, Kadja, Jane Keckley, Isabelle Keith, Nora Kildare, Lydia Knott, Alice

THE KING OF KINGS (1927): Muriel McCormack (left) as the Blind Girl.

41

THE KING OF KINGS (1927): The Crucifixion.

Knowland, Celia Lapan, Alla Moskova, Gertrude Norman, Patricia Palmer, Gertrude Quality, Rae Randall, Hedwig Reicher, Reeks Roberts, Peggy Schaeffer, Evelyn Selbie, Semone Sergis, Anne Teeman, Barbara Tennant, Mabel Van Buren, Stanhope Wheatcroft.

COMMENTARY

Few movie directors have been as successful commercially—or as repeatedly maligned critically—as Cecil B. DeMille. An evaluation of

object not so much to the premise that his spectacle films (which, after all, represent only a small portion of his varied output) were made badly, than to the fact that subject matter of this type was filmed at all. True, there have been more "intellectual" spectacles than DeMille's, but his detractors seem unaware (or unwilling to admit) that the often simplified dialogue and larger-than-life emotional attitudes in his films—especially in his period epics—represent an intentional style, an effort to make the people and events of remote eras more accessible to the modern viewer. To be sure, DeMille has faults. The budgets for his films seem to be unevenly distributed at times, resulting in an incongruously cheap scene or two per film, and DeMille's incessant moralizing and frequent lapses into vulgarity are irritating, but few other period films are as well researched and as accurate in costuming and architecture as his, and none have finer pictorial values, such a precise, instinctive sense of dramatically effective visual composition and lighting.

The most elaborate silent film adaptation of Christ's life, DeMille's *The King of Kings* is a textbook example of the director's virtues and faults. The film begins on an alarmingly lurid note as a scantily-clad Jacqueline Logan, portraying Mary Magdalene, entertains several of her male acquaintances in an opulent marble pleasure palace. Not only does this scene reveal a degree of cynicism on DeMille's part (apparently, he felt that only the quick introduction of sex would grip and hold the audience), but it also serves the purpose of establishing an unconvincing romantic triangle involving Mary, her lover Judas Iscariot, and Jesus. A peeved Mary is informed that the absent Judas has joined Christ's Disciples and flounces off in her chariot to confront Jesus. Here the film suddenly and jarringly shifts its thematic gears, as if DeMille realized his error, and becomes a simple presentation of Christ's life, reverently and imaginatively filmed.

H. B. Warner as Jesus is dramatically introduced when a blind girl, appealing to him for help, is miraculously cured, her sight restored. Warner is first shown from the girl's point of view as she regains her vision, a single ray of

DeMille's filmography and the often adverse critical reaction to his work leaves one with the impression that his chief offense has been producing consistently profitable entertainment for a mass audience. DeMille's critics, often unreasonable in their charges, seem to

light gradually dissolving into an impressive close-up of the actor. This scene, and the many other visually imaginative ones in the film, represent DeMille at his best. Warner's acting throughout is impeccable; as Jesus he is a virile, charismatic figure, both convincingly human and convincingly divine. After this scene, Mary Magdalene arrives, intending to denounce Jesus, but is instead converted when, in a richly symbolic double-exposure, she is cleansed of the Seven Deadly Sins, which abandon her form one at a time, each still attempting to seduce her. From this point on-

ward *The King of Kings* proceeds at a steady pace, with the improbable romance between the principals wisely downplayed.

The Crucifixion scene is spectacular, with its convincing storm and multitudes of extras obliterated in apocalyptic earth tremors, and the Resurrection, beautifully filmed in two-strip Technicolor, brings the film to an emotionally-charged dramatic peak at its conclusion. Regardless of its flawed narrative structure and occasional lapses into bad taste, DeMille's *The King of Kings* is one of the best religious pictures ever filmed, and certainly

44   THE KING OF KINGS (1927): The Last Supper.

one of the most successful adaptations of Jesus's life attempted by Hollywood. *The King of Kings* was so widely seen, and occasionally shown on television well into the 1970s, that another major film version of Christ's life was not produced until the similarly titled *King of Kings* in 1961. DeMille's film was reissued in 1931 with a synchronized music score and sound-effects track.

REVIEWS

Hardly a whispered word was uttered among the audience . . . . This long series of animated scenes, with its fine settings, adequate costumes and uniforms and its host of players, is an extraordinary and unprecedented film undertaking. Mr. DeMille has not satisfied himself with the mere action of the story, but he has endeavored in various ways to depict the characteristics of the Twelve Apostles and others, and in more than one instance he has set forth incidents in an inspired fashion.

New York Times

. . . This DeMille celluloid monument will be a super-production for years to come.

Variety

MORE FILMS OF THE 1920s

In *The Man Who Dared*, a six-reel feature released by Fox on August 29, 1920, a man (William Russell) wrongly accused of murder is sentenced to prison. He watches as, in a nearby cell, an Italian stonecutter, convicted of murder and sentenced to death, spends his last night on earth sculpting a figure of Jesus. When the stonecutter collapses from exhaustion, the spirit of Christ appears and comforts the prisoner. New evidence is then discovered, proving the alleged robber's innocence. The film was directed by Emmett J. Flynn from a screenplay by Julius J. Furthman.

A similar plot unfolded in *The Great Redeemer*, released by Metro on October 18, 1920. This six-reeler was directed by Clarence Brown

THE KING OF KINGS (1927): Jacqueline Logan as Mary Magdalene.

from a screenplay by H. H. Van Loan, Jules Furthman, and future matinee idol John Gilbert. A convicted robber (House Peters) serving time in prison sketches a figure of Christ on the wall of his cell; a condemned murderer (Joseph Singleton) in an adjoining cell sees the figure come to life and repents before his execution.

The Servant in the House (Federated, 1921) told an allegorical story involving the wealthy Bishop of Benares (Jean Hersholt), who disguises himself as a servant in order to observe his brother, the Vicar of a struggling church. The Bishop, resembling Jesus Christ, influences the lives of those around him through his kindness and generosity. Jack Conway directed under the name Hugh Ryan Conway, and Lanier Bartlett based his screenplay for this five-reel feature on a 1908 play by Charles Rann Kennedy. The film initially had been scheduled for release by FBO in 1920, and was trimmed from its original nine reels.

Leaves From Satan's Book (Nordisk, 1921), directed by Carl Theodor Dreyer, was a seven-reel horror fantasy made in Denmark containing four separate episodes; in each, Satan claims the soul of a person in a different historical era. One of the stories involves Jesus Christ (played by Halvard Hoff), and Satan's unsuccessful attempt to corrupt him. This film was based on a novel by Marie Corelli, which also inspired D. W. Griffith's 1925 Paramount feature *The Sorrows of Satan* (in which Christ did not appear).

A lost film, *Crusade of the Innocent* (Jawitz, 1922) was a five-reel exploitation picture described in the *New York Times* as "a story of leprosy (or syphilis), seduction, murder, and cruelty, and final redemption—with close-ups of Jesus Christ in all the art titles."

I. N. R. I. (Neumann, 1923), a seventy-minute German film, was directed by Robert Weine, who four years earlier had given the cinema one of its landmark films, *The Cabinet of Dr. Caligari*. Weine's *I. N. R. I.* told the story of Jesus (Gregori Chmara) as related to a convicted murderer on the night before his execution. Produced as a vehicle for Danish actress Asta Nielsen, who played Mary Magdalene and was married to Chmara, *I. N. R. I.* was reissued in 1934 as *Crown of Thorns*, with an added soundtrack of music and narration. The film's biblical scenes were shot on location in Palestine.

Respected stage actress Alla Nazimova produced and starred in a new version of *Salomé* (Allied, 1923), based on the stylized drawings by Aubrey Beardsley appearing in the first published edition of Oscar Wilde's play. Photographed by Charles Van Enger and designed by Natasha Rambova (the second wife of Rudolph Valentino), the film is visually stunning but achieves little more than pictorial artifice. The movie's dramatic shallowness and the pretentious emoting of its star were noted even in 1922, and *Salomé* was ignored by the public. Nazimova, who had invested heavily in the production, lost a great deal of money on this unsuccessful six-reel epic, which *Photoplay* magazine described as "A hot house [sic] orchid of decadent passion." The film was re-vived—to amused response—by film archivist Raymond Rohauer at a 1967 Beardsley retrospective at the Museum of Modern Art in New York. With its ethereal visuals, *Salomé* appeared to viewers forty-five years later very much like a relic from another world. A competing low-budget version of *Salomé*, actually released six weeks earlier than the Nazimova picture, was produced and directed by Malcolm Strauss, with Diana Allen in the lead. George H. Wiley, Inc., released the six-reel picture on New Year's Day 1923.

The Wandering Jew (Stoll, 1923) was an eight-reel British production of the familiar story, directed by Maurice Elvey and starring Matheson Lang. Although scenarist Alicia Ramsey derived her script from the play by E. Temple Thurston instead of the original Eugene Sue novel, Thurston had been true to the source, and the story conformed to earlier versions (a 1921 film entitled *The Wandering Jew* has no relation at all to either the Sue novel or the Thurston play).

A forty-five-minute version of *The Passion Play*, directed by Dimitri Buchowetzki and released by Gospel Films in 1924, was based on the Da Vinci painting *The Last Supper*. A filmed record of the Frieburg, Germany, Passion Play, this featurette starred Adolph Fassnacht as Jesus; Fassnacht's family had performed in the Frieburg Passion Play for generations.

Produced on location in Palestine, *The Man Nobody Knows*, a six-reel feature released by Pictorial Clubs in November of 1925, was based on the popular book *The Man Nobody Knows: A Discovery of Jesus* by Bruce Barton, who also wrote the titles for the film. Directed and photographed by Errett LeRoy Kenepp [sic], the picture dramatized the story of Jesus's life, interspersing these scenes with documentary footage of the Holy Land. The musical score for the film, using traditional hymns and spirituals, was arranged by Alexander Savine.

A new version of *Quo Vadis?*, produced in Italy and directed by Arturo Ambrosio, was released by First National in 1925. Starring Emil Jannings as Nero, the film was exhibited in two parts, with the most spectacular scenes reserved for the second half. Its huge budget aside, the ten-reel epic was not well received, and *Variety* felt that the film "does not stand out as anything remarkable. The industry has gone forward tremendously since the first *Quo Vadis?* was made, but in this present picture one does not find any great exposition of the advancement. *Quo Vadis?*, while a big picture in a way, is not one that is going to set the country afire . . ." The film was reissued, with a synchronized music score, in 1929.

Directed by Raoul Walsh and photographed by Victor Milner, *The Wanderer*, with original prints color-tinted, was released by Paramount on February 1, 1926. The nine-reel feature related the biblical parable of the Prodigal Son and starred Greta Nissen and William Collier, Jr. The screenplay by James T. O'Donahue was based on a stage adaptation by Maurice V. Samuels.

Jesus of Nazareth, released in March 1928 by Ideal Pictures, was a six-reel production dramatizing the life of Christ, starring Philip Van Loan as Jesus and Anna Lehr as the Virgin Mary. A low-budget offering, it was edited and

JESUS OF NAZARETH (1928): The Last Supper.

JESUS OF NAZARETH (1928): Philip Van Loan.

JESUS OF NAZARETH (1928)

titled by Jean Conover, and existing stills show at least one exceptionally lavish scene, prompting speculation that some portions of the film may have been lifted from a more elaborate European production.

In *Motherhood: Life's Greatest Miracle* (Blue Ray Prods., 1928), opening scenes of the Christ child in the manger segue into an anti-abortion drama contrasting the opposing reactions of two pregnant women—one wealthy, the other poor—to their approaching motherhood. Scripted by Lita Lawrence, the film had a 1925 copyright, but was not released until three years later.

Another version of *The Passion Play*, in a feature-length format, also was released in 1928. The picture was distributed by The Passion Play Committee for church and educational showings.

JESUS OF NAZARETH (1928): The Crucifixion.

JESUS OF NAZARETH (1928):
The Nativity.

JESUS OF NAZARETH (1928)

JESUS OF NAZARETH (1928): Philip Van Loan as Jesus, carrying his cross.

CHAPTER 3

THE NINETEEN THIRTIES

DESTINATION UNKNOWN

1933 Universal

CREDITS

Director: Tay Garnett; *Screenplay:* Thomas Buckingham; *Photography:* Edward Snyder; *Film Editor:* Milton Carruth. *Running Time:* 65 minutes.

CAST

Pat O'Brien (*Matt Brennan*); Ralph Bellamy (*The Stowaway*); Alan Hale (*Lundstrom*); Russell Hopton (*Georgie*); Tom Brown (*Johnny*); Betty Compson (*Ruby Smith*); Noel Madison (*Maxie*); Stanley Fields (*Gattallo*); Rollo Lloyd (*Dr. Fram*); Willard Robertson (*Joe Shane*); Charles Middleton (*Turk*); Richard Alexander (*Alex*); Forrester Harvey (*Ring*); George Rigas (*Tauru*).

COMMENTARY

In this bizarre feature, a rum-running cargo ship is becalmed in the Pacific, out of supplies, and in danger of sinking, with bo'sun Alan Hale left in charge of the desperate crew after the captain and first mate have been lost at sea.

A mysterious, nameless stowaway (Ralph Bellamy) appears onboard and uses implied supernatural powers to aid the crew and passengers. The script infers that the stowaway is Jesus Christ, and screenwriter Thomas Buckingham indulges in a deft bit of reverse allegory when the Bellamy character informs the crew, dying of thirst, that the kegs onboard thought to hold wine are actually full of fresh water—supposedly placed in them by a crooked trader!

In its general plot and allegorical details, the film recalls *The Passing of the Third Floor Back* and other silent morality plays, and it is also very similar to MGM's later *Strange Cargo*, seeming almost like a blueprint for that Joan Crawford–Clark Gable vehicle. Although the cast of *Destination Unknown* is good, and the early portion of the film is atmospheric and effective, the picture was not a success and is seldom, if ever, screened today. Director Tay Garnett once said of it: "In spite of an excellent script and a brilliant cast . . . *Destination Unknown* should have been titled *Destination Oblivion.* It sank without a trace."

DESTINATION UNKNOWN: Betty Compson and Pat O'Brien.

REVIEW

"A strange concoction, parts of which appear to have been written on the spur of the moment to fill in the necessary footage. . . . Although it has a certain fund of originality, it is spasmodically illogical and bewildering.

New York Times

THE LAST DAYS OF POMPEII

1935 RKO Radio

CREDITS

Director: Ernest B. Schoedsack; *Producer:* Merian C. Cooper; *Screenplay:* Ruth Rose, Boris Ingster (*based on a story by* James Ashmore Creelman and Melville Baker); *Photography:* Eddie Linden, Jr., Ray Hunt; *Music:* Roy Webb; *Film Editor:* Archie Marshek; *Special Effects:* Willis O'Brien, Vernon Walker, Harry Richmond. *Running Time:* 96 minutes.

CAST

Preston Foster (*Marcus*); Alan Hale (*Burbix*); Basil Rathbone (*Pontius Pilate*); John Wood (*Flavius as a Man*); Louis Calhern (*Prefect*); David Holt (*Flavius as a Boy*); Dorothy Wilson (*Clodia*); Wyrley Birch (*Leaster*); Gloria Shea (*Julia*); Frank Conroy (*Gaius*); William V. Mong (*Cleon*); Edward Van Sloan (*Calvus*); Henry Kolker (*Warder*); Zeffie Tilbury (*Wise Woman*); WITH John Davidson, Ward Bond, Edwin Maxwell, Oscar Apfel, Dutch Hendrian, Rodney Hildebrand.

COMMENTARY

From RKO and Merian C. Cooper, the studio and producer of *King Kong,* came *The Last Days of Pompeii* in 1935. The film borrowed not much more than the title from the classic novel by Edward Bulwer-Lytton. Although the volcano Vesuvius actually erupted, destroying Pompeii, in 79 A. D., scenarists Ruth Rose and Boris Ingster shifted the historical facts a bit and moved the disaster back a few decades to roughly coincide with the Crucifixion of Jesus.

A blacksmith named Marcus (Preston Foster) becomes a gladiator after his wife and child die under the wheels of a nobleman's chariot. Obsessed with the pursuit of wealth, he nevertheless adopts Flavius, the son of a fellow gladiator killed in the arena. Marcus is wounded in combat, and the crippled gladiator turns to slave trading as an alternate profession. Pontius Pilate (Basil Rathbone), aware of Marcus's reputation as a mercenary, secretly employs him as a horse thief, but Marcus's adopted son is injured in a raid. Jesus Christ heals the boy, and when Marcus leaves Judea with Flavius, they witness the Crucifixion from afar, unaware of the event's true significance. Several years pass, with Marcus gaining wealth and influence until he commands the arena in Pompeii. When the now grown Flavius, who has become a Christian, is captured and thrown into the arena with other prisoners condemned to death, Marcus finally realizes the error of his ways and tries to save the martyrs, just as Vesuvius erupts. Sacrificing himself in order to release his son and the other Christians, Marcus perishes in the violent fire-

THE LAST DAYS OF POMPEII (1935): Dutch Hendrian (left), Ward Bond (in helmet), William V. Mong (in toga), and Rodney Hildebrand (right).

storm engulfing the city, but as he dies, he is blessed by a vision of Jesus Christ.

The Last Days of Pompeii, although historically inaccurate, is an entertaining action film, and contains a wonderfully modulated performance from Basil Rathbone as Pilate, communicating a genuine sense of pained remorse and furtive guilt over the procurator's fateful decision to crucify Jesus. The figure of Christ in the film, played by an unbilled actor, is glimpsed only briefly, as a shadow or (in the conclusion) a transparent apparition. The special effects, involving miniatures and optical printing, are by the same technical crew responsible for *King Kong*, and provide an amazing illusion of carnage and mass destruction. Originally planned as a Technicolor feature, the film had sets and costumes designed for color photography, and a day's worth of Technicolor test footage was actually shot before studio executives decided to economize with black-and-white photography. Ironically, the feature was later computer-colored for showings by Turner Network Television. The 1960 Italian remake using the same title, starring Steve Reeves and Christine Kaufmann, also

THE LAST DAYS OF POMPEII (1935): Preston Foster (left), Gloria Shea, and Wyrley Birch. Young David Holt is on the bed.

THE LAST DAYS OF POMPEII (1935): Preston Foster (left).

THE LAST DAYS OF POMPEII (1935): Preston Foster as
Marcus, flanked by Wyrley Birch and Oscar Apfel.

THE LAST DAYS OF POMPEII (1935): Chaos during the
volcanic eruption.

THE LAST DAYS OF POMPEII (1960): Steve Reeves and
Christine Kaufmann in the remake.

deserves mention since it retained the Christian motif of the 1935 film, although Christ was not seen in this version. For the record, hyperactive Vesuvius also spewed forth moral retribution in such Italian movies as *The Rivals: A Love Drama of Pompeii* (1908), *The Last Days of Pompeii* (1908), and *The Martyr of Pompeii* (1909). In addition, there were *three* different Italian films entitled *The Last Days of Pompeii* in competition during 1913 (one directed by Mario Caserini), an elaborate remake with the same title in 1926, *The Sins of Pompeii* in 1955, and an all-star television miniseries, *The Last Days of Pompeii*, in 1985.

REVIEWS

Although it is persuasively staged and excitingly narrated, the work is rather more absorbing in its straightforward melodrama than in the later phases when the defiant gladiator is getting religion.

New York Times

THE LAST DAYS OF POMPEII (1935): John Wood (second from left, foreground) and Dorothy Wilson.

THE LAST DAYS OF POMPEII (1935)

THE LAST DAYS OF POMPEII (1935): Pilate (Basil Rathbone, left) and the gladiator Marcus (Preston Foster).

The Last Days of Pompeii is a spectacle picture, full of action and holds a good tempo throughout. . . . Basil Rathbone comes very close to stealing the picture with his playing of Pontius Pilate, the aristocrat not entirely without a conscience, who washes his hands of the blood of Jesus while tossing Him to the mob.

Variety

MORE FILMS OF THE 1930s

At least two more versions of *The Passion Play* were released in the early 1930s. One was shot as a silent for church and educational use and incorporated a staging of The Last Supper; the other version, distributed to churches and theaters by Screen Art Sales Co., was a filming of the Oberammergau Passion Play that had been

shot at least a decade earlier, with a sound track added.

Director Maurice Elvey remade his 1923 film of *The Wandering Jew* under the same title for Great Britain's Twickenham Film Studios in 1935. As in the earlier version, the script (by H. Fowler Mear) was based on the play by E. Temple Thurston. Incisive German actor Conrad Veidt starred in the title role, and the *New York Times* called the film "a rich and well-photographed production that moves steadily, if slowly, to a strongly dramatic climax."

Produced and written by Julien Duvivier, *Golgotha* (Film Union, 1935) was a French production starring Robert Le Vignan as Jesus and

featuring Jean Gabin as Pontius Pilate. Also known under the title *Ecce Homo* (*Behold the Man*), it is an expertly directed film shot on a $350,000 budget and the first sound movie adaptation of Christ's life. In its review, *Variety* hailed *Golgotha* as "an accomplishment that should bring world-wide prestige to the French film industry."

The Passing of the Third Floor Back (Gaumont, 1936), from Great Britain, was a new film version of the Jerome K. Jerome play, directed by Berthold Viertel, with Conrad Veidt and Anna Lee heading the cast. *Variety* noted, "Out of the film's happy combination of talents there develops a fine sustaining of mood and tempo,

THE LAST DAYS OF POMPEII (1935): Basil Rathbone as Pontius Pilate.

a background that makes the action feasible and a group of characterizations that impel recognition and interest."

Triumph, a 1937 British feature distributed by World Commonwealth Films, was a pseudo-documentary presenting scenes from the lives of key historical figures, including Jesus Christ, Leonardo Da Vinci, Abraham Lincoln, Socrates, and St. Francis of Assisi. The film was not distributed in America.

Prince of Peace (1939), a twenty-three-minute short subject distributed by GB Instructional, was another interpretation of the Nativity, directed by Donald Carter.

THE LAST DAYS OF POMPEII (1935): The volcano erupts.

THE LAWTON STORY

58

CHAPTER 4

THE NINETEEN FORTIES

STRANGE CARGO

1940 Metro-Goldwyn-Mayer

CREDITS

Director: Frank Borzage; *Producer:* Joseph L. Mankiewicz; *Screenplay:* Lawrence Hazard, Lester Samuels (*based on the book* Not Too Narrow . . . Not Too Deep *by* Richard Sale, *adapted by* Anita Loos); *Photography:* Robert Planck; *Music:* Franz Waxman; *Film Editor:* Robert J. Kern; *Art Director:* Cedric Gibbons. *Running Time:* 105 minutes.

CAST

Clark Gable (*André Verne*); Joan Crawford (*Julie*); Ian Hunter (*Cambreau*); Peter Lorre (*Cochon*); Paul Lukas (*Hessler*); Albert Dekker (*Moll*); J. Edward Bromberg (*Flaubert*); Eduardo Ciannelli (*Telez*); Victor Varconi (*Fisherman*); John Arledge (*Dufond*); Frederic Worlock (*Grideau*); Paul Fix (*Benet*); Bernard Nedell (*Marfeu*); Frances McDonald (*Moussenq*); Betty Compson (*Suzanne*); Charles Judels (*Renard*); Jack Mulhall (*Dunning*); Dewey Robinson (*Georges*); Harry Cording, Richard Alexander, Bud Fine, James Pierce, Hal Wynants, Christian Frank, Mitchell Lewis, Stanley Andrews, Dick Cramer, Ray Teal, Jack Adair (*Guards*); Gene Coogan, Eddie Foster, Frank Lackteen, Harry Samuels (*Convicts*); Art Dupuis (*Orderly*); Stanley Andrews (*Constable*); William Edmunds (*Watchman*).

COMMENTARY

The allegorical plot of *Strange Cargo* involves a group of convicts who, escaping from Devil's Island with a dance hall girl in tow, are accompanied by a mysterious figure presumed to be Jesus Christ. Although the focal character is the stranger (well-played by Ian Hunter, in a role originally intended for Melvyn Douglas), the stars are Joan Crawford (as the dancer) and, in his first movie after *Gone With the Wind* and his eighth with Crawford, Clark Gable (as a convict). Their dominating presence in the spotlight detracts somewhat from the overall effect. More emphasis should have been placed on Hunter, who is overshadowed even further by scene-stealing character actors like Peter Lorre and Eduardo Ciannelli. Still, the film is expertly crafted, and probably the best such allegory, with the sensitive direction by Frank Borzage and Robert Planck's careful, atmospheric cinematography reinforcing the

STRANGE CARGO: Clark Gable (flanked by Mitchell Lewis and Christian J. Frank) and Joan Crawford.

mood. Nevertheless, *Strange Cargo* was considered somewhat controversial in 1940. The Catholic Legion of Decency, which claimed that it "presents a naturalistic concept of religion contrary to the teachings of Christ, irreverent use of Scripture, and lustful implications in dialog and situations." The film's rating was later upgraded to "A-2" (unobjectionable for adults) after compliant MGM made a few adjusting cuts, but even so, the picture was still banned in Detroit and Providence, as well as in many other cities.

Joan Crawford was wisely deglamorized for her down-to-earth role, and according to studio publicity, her sparse wardrobe of three plain dresses cost only $40.

REVIEWS

Direction by Frank Borzage fails to hit the dramatic punches. His seems to be a delayed delivery that disappoints on the whole. He has not clearly defined the spiritual redemption angle which also adds to the audience confusion.

Variety

As it stands, the allegory is certainly not too deep, but it does seem a bit too narrow to accommodate itself readily to the broad and brutal sweep of the penny-dreadful narrative.

New York Times

THE GREAT COMMANDMENT

1942 20th Century-Fox

CREDITS

Director: Irving Pichel; *Producer:* John T. Coyle;

STRANGE CARGO: Clark Gable (left) and Ian Hunter.

Screenplay: Dana Burnet; *Photography:* Charles P. Boyle; *Music:* Hans Salter, Walter Jurman; *Film Editor:* Ralph Dixon; *Art Director:* Edward Jewell. *Running Time:* 78 minutes.

CAST

John Beal (*Joel*); Maurice Moscovich (*Lamech*); Albert Dekker (*Longinus*); Marjorie Cooley (*Tamar*); Warren McCullum (*Zadok*); Lloyd Corrigan (*Jemuel*); Ian Wolfe (*Tax Collector*); Olaf Hytten (*Nathan*); Anthony Marlowe (*Singer*); Lester Scharff (*First Zealot*); Albert Spehr (*Second Zealot*); Marc Loebell (*Judas*); Harold Minjir (*Andrew*); Earl Gunn (*Wounded Man*); George Rosener (*Merchant*); John Merton (*Under Officer*); Perry Evans (*First Elder*); Stanley Price (*Second Elder*); D'Arcy Corrigan (*Blind Man*); Max Davidson (*Old Man*).

COMMENTARY

Produced by Rev. James K. Friedrich's Cathedral Films in late 1939, *The Great Command-ment* was purchased by 20th Century-Fox with the intention of remaking it as a Tyrone Power vehicle. When the Power film was canceled, Fox simply released the original under its own studio logo. The movie, starring John Beal and Albert Dekker, is a drama of Christians opposing Romans in 30 A.D., and follows Christ and his Disciples as they spread the Gospel to their brethren. Although Jesus is not seen onscreen, his voice (eloquently dubbed by director Irving Pichel, who was also an actor) is heard off-camera.

The film's religious theme is undermined somewhat by the intrusion of a contrived romance. John Beal is featured as Joel, a young man leading a rebellion against the Roman Empire. His brother Longinus (Albert Dekker) is married to Tamar (Marjorie Cooley), whom Beal secretly loves. When a Roman soldier kills Longinus, Joel and Tamar are free to admit their love for each other, and influenced by

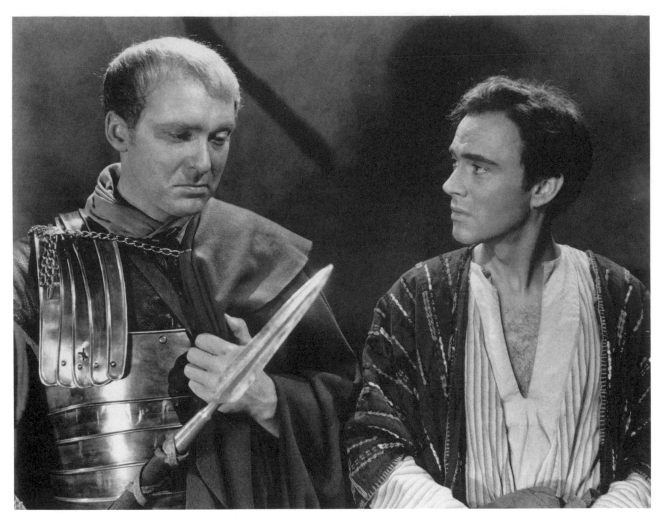

THE GREAT COMMANDMENT: Albert Dekker (left) and John Beal.

Christianity, they reject the violence of the revolution.

REVIEW

As a religious film which has been gathering dust on the shelves of Twentieth Century-Fox for three years or more, its only virtue is the restrained reverence with which it includes the figure of Jesus.

New York Times

Dealing with early Christian days and the oppression of Roman rule, it is a religious document which possesses some interest, though as entertainment it measures up poorly . . . Love for thy neighbor and other teachings of the Carpenter of Nazareth form the basis for the picture, with a romance thrown in that fails to provide much strength.

Variety

THE LAWTON STORY

1949 Hallmark

CREDITS

Directors: William Beaudine, Harold Daniels; *Producer:* Kroger Babb; *Screenplay:* Scott Darling, De Vallon Scott (*based on stories by* Milton Raison, Mildred A. Horn, Rev. A. Mark Wallock); *Photography* (*Cinecolor*): Henry Sharp; *Music Director:* Edward J. Kay; *Lyrics:* Lee "Lasses" White, Steven Edwards, Andy Page, Vachel Lindsey; *Film Editor:*

THE LAWTON STORY: Millard Coody as Jesus.

THE LAWTON STORY: Millard Coody (right).

Dick Currier; *Art Director:* Dave Milton. *Running Time:* 101 minutes.

CAST

Millard Coody played *Jesus* (and himself) in a cast that included: Ginger Prince (*Ginger*); Forrest Taylor (*Uncle Mark*); Ferris Taylor (*Uncle Jonathan*); Maude Eburne (*Henrietta*); Gwyn Shipman (*Jane*); Darlene Bridges (*Herself/Virgin Mary*); Willa Pearl Curtis (*Willa Pearl*); Ray Largay (*Dr. Martin*); A. S. Fischer (*Himself/Simon*); Hazel Lee Becker (*Herself/Mary Magdalene*); Knox Manning (*Narrator*); WITH Lee "Lasses" White.

COMMENTARY

The Lawton Story was produced by Kroger Babb, a prolific distributor of independently financed low-budget exploitation fare. Shot in Lawton, Oklahoma, the feature was shown in two parts with an intermission, and told of the town's annual Passion Play, originated in 1926 by Rev. Mark Wallock, minister of the Lawton Congregational Church. The first half of the film, photographed in weak "Natural Color," shows Lawton's plans for staging the Passion Play and the effects of the preparation on the citizens. The second half, filmed in Cinecolor, depicts the actual play, involving the town's

THE LAWTON STORY: Jesus (Millard Coody) speaks to his followers.

3,000 inhabitants and performed in a huge mountain amphitheater. The citizens of Lawton portray themselves, as well as their assigned biblical roles, with Millard Coody playing Jesus. As a social document, the film's second half is of genuine value and interest, but the introductory segment is contrived, with too much footage expended on Ginger Prince, a vivacious youngster spotlighted by the producer. *The Lawton Story* was reissued in 1951 as *The Prince of Peace*.

REVIEWS

It would have been a finer picture had not

instance sincerity is more important than technical perfection.

New York Times

MORE FILMS OF THE 1940s

Luis Alcoriza portrayed Jesus in *Mary Magdalene*, a 1946 Mexican feature directed by Miguel Torres, focusing on the biblical courtesan.

The Wandering Jew (*L'Ebreo Errante*) (Globe, 1947) was a liberal adaptation of the familiar legend produced in Italy, with Nazis included in the plotline. This version, directed by Goffredo Alessandrini, starred Vittorio Gassman and Valentina Cortese.

Which Will You Have? was a thirty-six minute featurette directed by Donald Taylor and released in July 1949 by Great Britain's GB In-

the producers seen fit to draw in a crass commercial showcasing of a precocious moppet, apparently in an attempt to strike a broader popular market. . . . The untutored simplicity with which the cast of townspeople go about their renewal of faith has a stirring emotional quality, the prime essential of all religious appeal.

Variety

The principal roles are played by residents of Lawton, and though their performances do not always reflect the full drama of the "greatest story ever told," they are sincere, and in this

THE LAWTON STORY: Millard Coody as Jesus.

THE LAWTON STORY: The Crucifixion.

THE LAWTON STORY: Millard Coody (right).

structional. It told the story of Barabbas, the thief who was pardoned and released from prison when Jesus was crucified. Nial McGinnis played Barabbas and Betty Ann Davies was cast as Mary Magdalene; in the U.S., the film was entitled *Barabbas the Robber*.

Also deserving of mention are the ambitious but unrealized projects of two great filmmakers: *The Divine Tragedy*, to have been shot by Abel Gance in 1949, and *Jesus of Nazareth*, an ill-fated production conceived by Carl Theodor Dreyer the same year. The unfilmed *Jesus of*

67

THE LAWTON STORY: Millard Coody
(center); the Last Supper.

Nazareth project (the screenplay for which has
been published in French and English) re-
mained something of an obsession with
Dreyer, who, after lengthy and futile negotia-
tions with American producer Blevins Davis,
refused to work on other religious films that
were offered to him. He persisted in seeking
backing for *Jesus of Nazareth* until his death on
March 20, 1968.

THE LAWTON STORY: **The Last Supper.**

THE LAWTON STORY: **Millard Coody (right).**

70

THE LAWTON STORY: **Jesus bearing his cross to Calvary.**

QUO VADIS? (1951): Robert Taylor (fourth from left), Deborah Kerr, and Buddy Baer, flanked by centurions.

CHAPTER 5

THE NINETEEN FIFTIES

QUO VADIS?

1951 Metro-Goldwyn-Mayer

CREDITS

Director: Mervyn LeRoy; *Producer:* Sam Zimbalist; *Screenplay:* John Lee Mahin, S. N. Behrman, Sonya Levien (*based on the novel by* Henryk Sankiewicz); *Photography* (*Technicolor*): Robert Surtees, William V. Skall; *Music:* Miklos Rozsa; *Film Editor:* Ralph E. Winters; *Art Directors:* William Horning, Cedric Gibbons, Edward Carfagno; *Set Designer:* Hugh Hunt; *Costumes:* Herschel McCoy; *Choreography:* Marta Obolensky, Auriel Millos; *Special Effects:* Thomas Howard, A. Arnold Gillespie, Donald Jahmaus; *Historical Advisor:* Hugh Gray. *Running Time:* 171 minutes.

CAST

Robert Taylor (*Marcus Vinicius*); Deborah Kerr (*Lygia*); Leo Genn (*Petronius*); Peter Ustinov (*Nero*); Patricia Laffan (*Poppaea*); Finlay Currie (*Peter*); Abraham Sofaer (*Paul*); Marina Berti (*Eunice*); Buddy Baer (*Ursus*); Felix Aylmer (*Plautius*); Nora Swinburne (*Pomponia*); Ralph Truman (*Tigellinus*); Norman Wooland (*Nerva*); Peter Miles (*Nazarius*); Geoffrey Dunn (*Terpnos*); Nicholas Hannen (*Seneca*); D. A. Clark Smith (*Phaon*); Rosalie Crutchley (*Acte*); John Ruddock (*Chilo*); Arthur Walge (*Croton*); Elspeth March (*Miriam*); Strelsa Brown (*Rufia*); Alfredo Varelli (*Lucan*); Roberto Ottaviano (*Flavius*); William Tubbs (*Anaxander*); Pietro Tordi (*Galba*); Lia Deleo (*Pedicurist*); Sophia Loren, Elizabeth Taylor (*Extras*); Walter Pidgeon (*Narrator*).

COMMENTARY

Produced at a then-impressive cost of $7 million and shot in Italy over a period of six months, this was the third major film version of the Henryk Sankiewicz novel. The film, tightly directed by Mervyn LeRoy and starring Robert Taylor, Deborah Kerr, and Peter Ustinov, had been considered for Metro's production slate as far back as the 1930s, when studio producer Hunt Stromberg scouted locations in Italy, only to abandon the project with the outbreak of World War II. John Huston was to have directed another incarnation, starring Gregory Peck and Elizabeth Taylor, in 1949. Shooting had actually begun on Italian locations, with costs soaring to $2 million, before production faltered and collapsed, due both to the chaotic state of Italy's postwar film indus-

73

try and the internecine warfare between producer Dore Schary and MGM studio chief Louis B. Mayer (who was, of course, extremely pleased with the defeat of Schary, his rival for control of studio production). Mayer then launched his own version, with Sam Zimbalist as producer and LeRoy as director.

As film spectacles go, *Quo Vadis?* is unusually intelligent. Although, like the earlier versions, based on the Sankiewicz novel, the 1951 *Quo Vadis?* also owes a great deal to Cecil B. DeMille's 1932 *The Sign of the Cross*, particularly in Ustinov's effete interpretation of the Emperor Nero, played by Charles Laughton in the DeMille film. In comparing the two performances, Laughton has the edge (offering, with Claudette Colbert as Poppaea, a most convincing pre-Code illustration of Roman decadence), but Ustinov is formidable in his own right. His performance is so richly detailed

that, in spite of all of Nero's infamous crimes, the viewer almost pities him when he finally dies mad, alone, and innocently bewildered by his loss of power. Although Ustinov's delineation might be called by some as hammy as Laughton's, the role, in all its power-crazed, egocentric insanity, demands a larger-than-life treatment; underplaying would only disappoint. And (again, like Laughton before him), Ustinov undeniably steals every scene he appears in.

Robert Taylor as Marcus Vinicius, the hedonistic Roman soldier in love with Christian slave girl Lygia (Deborah Kerr), fares less well. Taylor makes a believable hero, but his character is sketchy and his acceptance of Christianity too quick and unconvincing. Kerr is appropriately beautiful, though, and Patricia Laffan as Poppaea and Finlay Currie as the Apostle Peter register well in their supporting roles. Jesus

THE SIGN OF THE CROSS: Charles Laughton as Nero.

74

QUO VADIS? (1951): Peter Ustinov as Nero.

Christ is shown briefly, in a flashback tableau depiction of the Last Supper, meticulously fashioned after the Da Vinci painting, as Peter delivers a sermon. Boasting vibrant Technicolor photography by Robert Surtees and William V. Skall, a fine music score by Miklos Rozsa (played in large part on instruments appropriate to the era), and a sprawling cast of 8,000 extras (including, it is said, a young Elizabeth Taylor and Sophia Loren), *Quo Vadis?* was a huge success, grossing $25 million worldwide and paving the way for the later religious epics of the 1950s.

QUO VADIS? (1951): Patricia Laffin as Poppaea.

THE SIGN OF THE CROSS: **Provocative Claudette Colbert as Poppaea.**

Leonardo da Vinci's masterpiece *THE LAST SUPPER* (painted 1495–97).

QUO VADIS? (1951): A painstakingly exact re-creation of da Vinci's painting, included as a flashback in the film.

QUO VADIS? (1951): Ralph Truman as Tigellinus.

REVIEWS

The scenes of Roman gatherings in Nero's decadent reign to honor triumphant heroes or to watch Christians clawed to death by lions are rendered intoxicating by the magnificence of the sets and the massing of thousands of extras, which shooting in Italy has allowed Metro to afford.

New York Times

There are shortcomings even Metro must have recognized and ignored in consideration of the project's scope. The captiousness about the story line and some of the players' wooden performances in contrast to the scenery-chewing of Peter Ustinov (Nero) are part and parcel of any super-spectacular. When the produc-tion values are so prodigious it is almost impossible for some of the other components to match them. In effect, the super-colossal handicapped the realistic values. If the histrionics, if portions of the script and segments of the direction prove spotty, it does not necessarily follow that there aren't as many highlights in acting, cinematurgy and directorial investiture.

Variety

I BEHELD HIS GLORY

1952 Cathedral Films

CREDITS

Director: John T. Coyle; *Producer:* Rev. James K. Friedrich, L.H.D.; *Screenplay:* Arthur T. Horman

QUO VADIS? (1951): Geoffrey Dunn as

I BELHELD HIS GLORY: Robert Wilson as Jesus at the Last Supper.

QUO VADIS? (1951): Buddy Baer (background), Deborah Kerr (left), and Robert Taylor. At right are Nora Swinburne and Peter Miles.

(*based on a story by* Rev. John Evans); *Photography (color):* Freddie West; *Music:* Irving Gertz; *Film Editor:* Tom Neff; *Makeup:* Larry Butterfield; *Sound:* William Randall, Joe Moss; *Production Manager:* Theodore Joos; *Script Supervisor:* Wesley Jones. *Running Time:* 55 minutes.

CAST

Robert Wilson played *Jesus* in a cast that included: George Macready (*Cornelius*); Lowell Gilmore (*Pilate*); James Flavin (*Longinus*); Grandon Rhoades (*Eltheas*); Thomas Charlesworth (*Thomas*); Morris Ankrum (*Peter*); Stan Jolley (*Dismus*); Virginia Wave (*Mary Magdalene*).

COMMENTARY

This noteworthy independent production told the story of Jesus in flashback. A Roman centurion (George Macready) who had witnessed the events relates the story of Christ to a relative of the Disciple Thomas. Although the film is unimaginative and stolidly directed by John T. Coyle, Robert Wilson, who later would

essay the role in the 1954 feature *Day of Tri-umph*, was fine as Jesus, and the cast also included such familiar Hollywood character actors as James Flavin, Morris Ankrum, and I. Stanford Jolley.

SALOMÉ

1953 Columbia

CREDITS

Director: William Dieterle; *Producer:* Buddy Adler; *Screenplay:* Harry Kleiner (*based on a story by* Jesse Lasky, Jr., Harry Kleiner); *Photography* (*Technicolor*): Charles Lang; *Music:* George Duning, Daniel Amfitheatrof; *Music Direction:* Morris W. Stoloff; *Film Editor:* Viola Lawrence; *Art Direction:* John Meehan; *Set Designer:* William Kiernan; *Costumes:* Jean Louis, Emile Santiago; *Choreography:* Valerie Bettis; *Makeup:* Clay Campbell; *Religious Technical Advisor:* Millard Sheets. *Running Time:* 103 minutes.

SALOMÉ (1953): Rita Hayworth as Salomé.

SALOMÉ (1953): Rita Hayworth as Salomé.

CAST

Rita Hayworth (*Princess Salomé*); Stewart Granger (*Commander Claudias*); Charles Laughton (*King Herod*); Judith Anderson (*Queen Herodias*); Sir Cedric Hardwicke (*Caesar Tiberius*); Alan Badel (*John the Baptist*); Basil Sydney (*Pontius Pilate*); Maurice Schwartz (*Ezra*); Rex Reason (*Marcellus Fabius*); Arnold Moss (*Micha*); Sujata and Asoka (*Oriental Dance Team*); Robert Warwick (*Courier*); Carmen D'Antonio (*Salomé's Servant*); Michael Granger (*Capt. Quintus*); Karl "Killer" Davis (*Slave Master*); Joe Schilling, David Wold, Ray Beltram, Joe Sawaya, Anton Northpole, Carlo Tricoli, Franz Roehn, William McCormick (*Advisors*); Mickey Simpson (*Herod's Captain of the Guards*); Eduardo Cansino (*Roman Guard*); Lou Nova (*Executioner*); Fred Letuli, John Wood (*Sword Dancers*); William Spaeth (*Fire Eater*); Abel Pina, Jerry Pina, Henry Pina, Henry Escalante, Gilbert Marques, Richard Rivas, Miguel Guitierez, Ramiro Rivas, Ruben T. Rivas, Hector Urtiaga (*Acrobats*); Duke Johnson (*Juggling Specialty*); Earl Brown, Bud Cokes (*Galilean Soldiers*); George Khoury, Leonard George (*Assassins*); Eva

Hyde (*Herodias's Servant*); Charles Wagenheim (*Simon*); Italia De Nubha, David Ahdar, Charles Soldani, Dimas Sotello, William Wilkerson, Mario Lamm, Tina Menard (*Converts*); Leslie Denison (*Court Attendant*); Henry dar Boggia, Michael Couzzi, Bobker Ben Ali, Don De Leo, John Parrish, Eddy Fields, Robert Garabedion, Sam Scar (*Politicians*); Tris Coffin, Bruce Cameron, John Crawford (*Guards*); Michael Mark (*Old Farmer*); David Leonard, Maurice Samuels, Ralph Moody (*Old Scholars*); Saul Martell (*Dissenting Scholar*); Paul Hoffman (*Sailmaster*); Stanley Waxman (*Patrician*); Franz Roehn, Jack Low, Bert Rose, Tom Hernandez (*Townsmen*); Trevor Ward (*Blind Man*); Barry Brooks (*Roman Guard*); Roque Barry (*Slave*); George Keymas, Fred Berest, Rick Vallin (*Sailors*); Carleton Young, Guy Kingsford (*Officers*).

COMMENTARY

Yet another version of the familiar Bible tale, this Columbia feature was mounted as a vehicle for an aging but still alluring Rita Hayworth, a decade past her *Gilda* prime and miscast in the role. Although the picture's apparent intent is to shock with a lurid tale, screenwriter Harry Kleiner, adapting frequent DeMille collaborator Jesse Lasky, Jr.'s story (to which Kleiner also contributed), failed to provide the required commercial ingredients, and was perhaps even told to downplay these exploitative factors in deference to Hayworth. As with Lana Turner's later *The Prodigal*, Hayworth's character is initially established as scandalous, but emerges as sympathetic before the fadeout. A very tame affair as a result, *Salomé* is remarkable more for its biblical distortions than for its effectiveness as a film.

The traditional plot was completely misrepresented by the screenwriters; this time Salomé dances to *save* John the Baptist, and when his decapitated head is presented to her, she flees King Herod's palace in disgust, joining her Roman lover (Stewart Granger) as they listen to Jesus deliver the Sermon on the Mount at the conclusion. A tedious picture hampered further by William Dieterle's lackluster direction, *Salomé* is partially redeemed by Charles Lang's excellent Technicolor photography and a hammy, eye-bulging performance from Charles Laughton as King Herod. Clearly realizing that his dramatic competition is a bit thin, Laughton interprets his character with relish, and does not disappoint, providing the movie's few enjoyable moments.

REVIEWS

More their own interpretation than a factual chronicle of the religious story, it is a vehicle especially slanted for Miss Hayworth, but injects such a wealth of material that the pace is methodical and tends to make William Dieterle's direction slow. Much more vigorous handling is needed to bring all of the footage to life.

Variety

A lush conglomeration of historical pretenses and make-believe, pseudo-religious os-

SALOMÉ (1953): Rita Hayworth, with Charles Laughton as Herod.

SALOMÉ (1953): Alan Badel as John the Baptist.

tentation and just plain insinuated sex. No one of moderate perception, observing the posters for this film, is likely to be deceived too greatly as to its biblical authenticity or its calculated provision of intellectual food. The billboard appearances of Miss Hayworth in various attitudes of repose, gowned in diaphanous garments and making with come-hither looks, suggest more profound enthusiasm for the delights of theatrical couture and the well-advertised allurements of a famous glamour queen.

New York Times

THE ROBE

1953 20th Century-Fox

CREDITS

Director: Henry Koster; *Producer:* Frank Ross; *Screenplay:* Philip Dunne (*based on the novel by* Lloyd C. Douglas, *adaptation by* Gina Kaus); *Photography (CinemaScope, Technicolor):* Leon Shamroy; *Music:* Alfred Newman; *Music Direction:* Edward Powell; *Film Editor:* Barbara McLean; *Art Direction:* Lyle Wheeler,

George W. Davis; *Special Effects:* Ray Kellogg. *Running Time:* 135 minutes.

CAST

Richard Burton (*Marcellus Gallio*); Jean Simmons (*Diana*); Victor Mature (*Demetrius*); Michael Rennie (*Peter*); Jay Robinson (*Caligula*); Dean Jagger (*Justus*); Torin Thatcher (*Senator Gallio*); Richard Boone (*Pilate*); Betta St. John (*Miriam*); Jeff Morrow (*Paulus*); Ernest Thesiger (*Emperor Tiberius*); Dawn Addams (*Junia*); Leon Askin (*Abidor*); Frank Pulaski (*Quintus*); David Leonard (*Marcipor*); Michael Ansara (*Judas*); Helen Beverly (*Rebecca*); Nicholas Koster (*Jonathan*); Francis Pierlot (*Dodinius*); Thomas Browne Henry (*Marius*); Anthony Eustrel (*Sarpe-* *don*); Pamela Robinson (*Lucia*); Jay Novello (*Tiro*); Emmett Lynn (*Nathan*); Sally Corner (*Cornelia*); Rosalind Ivan (*Julia*); George E. Stone (*Gracchus*); Marc Snow (*Auctioneer*); Mae Marsh (*Woman*); George Keymas (*Slave*); John Doucette (*Ship's Mate*); Ford Rainey, Sam Gilman (*Ship Captains*); Cameron Mitchell (*Voice of Christ*); Harry Shearer (*David*); Virginia Lee (*Specialty Dancer*); Leo Curley (*Shalum*); Jean Corbett, Joan Corbett, Gloria Saunders (*Slave Girls*); Percy Helton (*Caleb*); Roy Gordon (*Chamberlain*); Ben Astar (*Cleander*); WITH Frank De Kova, George Melford, Eleanor Moore, Irene Demetrion, Dan Ferniel, George Robotham, Alex Pope, Ed Mundy, Anthony Jochim, Van Des Autels, Hayden Rorke.

THE ROBE: Richard Burton (center) inspects the title garment.

COMMENTARY

20th Century-Fox's answer to the early 1950s threat of television was not necessarily better films with better scripts, but sheer size: literally bigger films on bigger screens. Alarmed by emptying movie houses, hence diminishing box office, studio head Darryl F. Zanuck gambled everything on an anamorphic optical process invented by Professor Henri Chretien. Patented as CinemaScope by the studio, the process optically "squeezed" the image as it was photographed, and a converse lens on the projector reversed the effect, resulting in a wide, panoramic rectangular vista filling a twenty-four- by sixty-eight-foot screen. Ignored were the legitimate concerns of cinematographers, who correctly argued that the new oblong ratio all but destroyed the art of picto-

THE ROBE: Victor Mature (standing) watches as Roman soldiers (with Richard Burton, fourth from the right) gamble for Jesus's robe.

rial composition and produced a murkier image due to the added lens elements. Ignored too were the complaints of harried exhibitors, already crippled by the impact of television and now forced to install new screens and projection lenses. At the time, though, and

THE ROBE: Richard Burton witnesses the Crucifixion.

strictly in a business sense, Zanuck was right. CinemaScope *did* save the studios and the industry, and when the first wide-screen films premiered, audiences were overwhelmed; the look of movies had been changed forever, in a more profitable if not more aesthetic way—first with Fox's process then with Panavision, WarnerScope, VistaVision, Superscope, etc.

For his studio's first offering in Cinema-Scope, Zanuck chose the Lloyd C. Douglas novel *The Robe*, purchasing the screen rights for $100,000. Produced at a cost of $8 million, *The Robe* is the story of Marcellus (Richard Burton), a Roman centurion ordered to crucify Jesus Christ. Indifferent to his actions, and even callously gambling with his fellow soldiers for Jesus's robe as his victim dies on the cross, Marcellus is startled when a violent storm erupts, and in the chaos, he sees his Greek slave Demetrius (Victor Mature) clutching Jesus's robe tearfully. Demetrius is later converted to Christianity by the Apostle Peter (Michael Rennie). Marcellus, in possession of Jesus's robe and questioning his own values, is influenced by his childhood sweetheart Diana (Jean Simmons), now a Christian, and he gradually embraces her beliefs. Ordered by the insane Emperor Caligula (Jay Robinson) to renounce Christ, Marcellus refuses, and is condemned to death with Diana. Before his execution, however, Marcellus passes the robe on to Demetrius's care.

With an excellent performance by Richard Burton (who appears in nearly every scene), *The Robe* was a huge success, quickly recouping its production costs. The film made an international star of Burton, until this time known primarily as a Shakespearean stage actor who dabbled in films and Jay Robinson also made a strong impression in a flamboyant, appropriately over-the-top performance as Caligula. In the Crucifixion scene, actor Cameron Mitchell provides the voice of Christ, glimpsed only fleetingly. Mitchell took the voice-over role in order to please his minister father, who disapproved of his son's show-business career.

REVIEWS

Twentieth Century-Fox removed the wrap-pings last night from its much-heralded Cine-maScope production of *The Robe* and revealed a historical drama less compelling than the process by which it is shown . . . . An unwavering force of personal drama is missed in the size and the length of the show . . . . When the music surges and swells from magnified multiple speakers that make up the system's stereophonic sound, the violent assault upon the senses dissipates spiritual intimacy.

New York Times

THE ROBE: Victor Mature as Demetrius.

The Robe, as a picture, has been ten years coming, first under RKO aegis when producer Frank Ross was there. It is a "big" picture in every sense of the word. One magnificent scene after another, under the anamorphic technique, unveils the splendor that was Rome and the turbulence that was Jerusalem at the time of Christ on Calvary.

Variety

DEMETRIUS AND THE GLADIATORS

1954 20th Century-Fox

CREDITS

Producer: Frank Ross; *Director:* Delmer Daves; *Screenplay:* Philip Dunne (*based on characters from the novel* The Robe *by Lloyd C. Douglas*); *Photography* (*CinemaScope, Deluxe Color*): Milton Krasner; *Music:* Franz Waxman; *Music Direction:* Alfred Newman; *Film Editors:* Dorothy Spencer, Robert Fritch; *Art Direction:* Lyle Wheeler, George W. Davis; *Costumes:* Charles LeMaire; *Special Effects:* Ray Kellogg; *Choreography:* Stephen Papick. *Running Time:* 101 minutes.

CAST

Victor Mature (*Demetrius*); Susan Hayward (*Messalina*); Michael Rennie (*Peter*); Debra Paget (*Lucia*); Anne Bancroft (*Paula*); Jay Robinson (*Caligula*); Barry Jones (*Claudius*); William Marshall (*Glycon*); Richard Egan (*Dardanius*); Ernest Borgnine (*Strabo*); Charles Evans (*Cassius Chaerea*); Everett Glass (*Kaeso*); Karl Davis (*Macro*); Jeff York (*Albus*); Carmen de Lavallade (*Slave Girl*); John Cliff (*Varus*); Barbara James, Willetta Smith (*Specialty Dancers*); Selmer Jackson (*Senator*); Douglas Brooks (*Cousin*); Fred Graham (*Decurion*); Dayton Lummis (*Magistrate*); George Eldredge (*Chamberlain*); Paul Richards (*Prisoner*); Ray Spiker, Gilbert Perkins, Paul Stader, Jim Winkler, Lyle Fox, Dick Sands, Woody Strode (*Gladiators*); Paul "Tiny" Newlan (*Potter*); Allan Kramer (*Clerk*); Paul Kruger (*Courtier*); George Bruggeman, William Forrest, Jack Finlay, Peter Mamakos, Shepard Menken, Harry Cording, and Richard Burton and Jean Simmons (*in footage from* The Robe).

COMMENTARY

This CinemaScope sequel to *The Robe* was partially filmed in conjunction with the first picture in order to minimize costs. Unlike its predecessor, *Demetrius and the Gladiators* (initially called simply *The Gladiators*) emphasized action at the expense of a religious theme, but taken on these more superficial terms, the film is well-done and effective. Director Delmer Daves keeps the picture moving at a brisk pace, and the DeLuxe Color photography of Milton Krasner is excellent. Victor Mature, Jay Robin-

DEMETRIUS AND THE GLADIATORS:
Susan Hayward, Victor
Mature, and John Cliff.

son, and Michael Rennie reprised their earlier roles, with Mature offering the same dense, beefcake performance that he contributed to *The Robe*. The spectacle's leading lady, Susan Hayward, although working with an ill-defined, sketchy characterization, is fine as the wicked Messalina, although some critics objected to what they saw as her excessively melodramatic performance. Debra Paget was given the second female lead as Lucia, and a

young Anne Bancroft was featured as a slave girl.

Jay Robinson pushed his interpretation of Caligula to new heights of insanity, maniacally ranting and raving through most of his scenes, and mincingly screeching "It won't work!" when he finally acquires the robe of Christ and the garment fails to restore life to a prisoner put to death by Caligula for just this purpose. Richard Egan, Ernest Borgnine, and particu-

90

larly William Marshall were also impressive in supporting roles. Richard Burton and Jean Simmons were seen at the beginning in a repeat of the closing scene of *The Robe* in order to bridge the two films.

REVIEWS

The Robe springboards this follow-up. . . . It is a completely new story, beautifully fashioned with all the basics of good drama and action that can play, and quite often do, against any setting, period or modern.

Variety

. . . They have millinered this saga along straight Cecil B. Devotional lines, which means stitching on equal cuttings of spectacle, action, sex and reverence.

New York Times

DEMETRIUS AND THE GLADIATORS: Caligula (Jay Robinson, left) confronts Demetrius (Victor Mature).

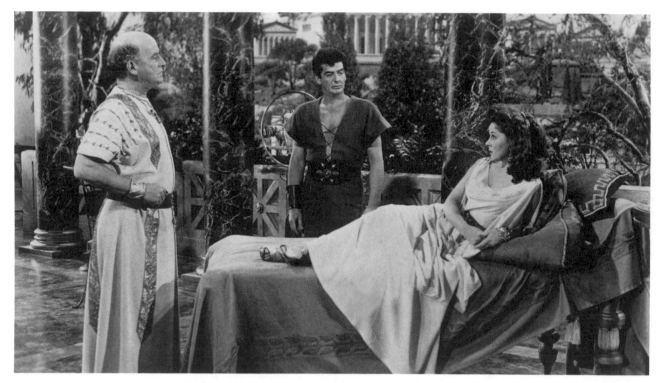

DEMETRIUS AND THE GLADIATORS: Demetrius listens as haughty Messalina shows disdain for her husband Claudius (Barry Jones, left), the future Caesar.

DEMETRIUS AND THE GLADIATORS: Victor Mature and Susan Hayward, flanked by Ernest Borgnine (left) and Barry Jones.

THE SILVER CHALICE

1954 Warner Bros.

CREDITS

Producer/Director: Victor Saville; *Screenplay:* Lester Samuels (*based on the novel by* Thomas B. Costain); *Photography (CinemaScope, Warnercolor):* William V. Skall; *Music:* Franz Waxman; *Film Editor:* George White; *Production Design and Costumes:* Rolf Gerard; *Art Director:* Boris Leven; *Choreography:* Stephen Papick. *Running Time:* 143 minutes.

CAST

Virginia Mayo (*Helena*); Jack Palance (*Simon*); Paul Newman (*Basil*); Pier Angeli (*Deborra*); Alexander Scourby (*Luke*); Joseph Wiseman (*Mijamin*); E. G. Marshall (*Ignatius*); Walter Hampden (*Joseph*); Jacques Aubuchon (*Nero*); Herbert Rudley (*Linus*); Albert Dekker (*Kester*); Michael Pate (*Aaron*); Lorne Greene (*Peter*); Terrence De Marney (*Sosthene*); Don Randolph (*Selech*); David Stewart (*Adam*); Phillip Tonge (*Ohad*); Ian Wolfe (*Therson*); Robert Middleton (*Idbash*); Mort Marshall (*Benjie*); Larry Dobkin (*Ephraim*); Natalie Wood (*Helena as a Girl*); Peter Reynolds (*Basil as a Boy*); Mel Welles (*Marcos*); Jack Raine (*Magistrate*); Beryl Machin (*Eulalia*); John Sheffield, John Marlowe, Paul Power (*Witnesses to Adoption*); Frank Hagney, Harry Wilson (*Ruffians*); Charles Bewley (*Roman Commander*); David Bond (*Cameleer*); Allen Michaelson (*High Priest*); Lester Sharpe (*Oasis Keeper*); Antony Eustral (*Maximus, the Ship's Master*); Laguna Festival of Art Players (*Tableau Performers*).

COMMENTARY

The Silver Chalice featured Paul Newman (in

THE SILVER CHALICE: Jack Palance and Virginia Mayo.

THE SILVER CHALICE: Virginia Mayo and Paul Newman.

THE SILVER CHALICE: Pier Angeli and Paul Newman.

his film debut) and Virginia Mayo in the melodramatic tale of a Greek sculptor who is assigned the task of molding a receptacle for the cup Jesus used at the Last Supper. Based on the best-selling novel by Thomas Costain, *The Silver Chalice* was produced at a cost of $4.5 million, and had nominal leading man Jack Palance contributing his excessive villainy and stealing the film in his role of Simon, a magician under the delusion that he can fly, and who, failing in the attempt, offers one of the picture's few memorable scenes. Future leading lady Natalie Wood also appears briefly, playing the Virginia Mayo character as a child. This picture remains something of an embarrassment for star Paul Newman (twenty-nine at the time), and when the film was eventually shown on television in Los Angeles for the first time, he actually placed newspaper ads apologizing for his performance. The Holy Grail, incidentally, was also used as a plot device in the 1989 big-budget action-adventure epic, *In-*

THE SILVER CHALICE: Paul Newman confronted by Lawrence Dobkin.

diana Jones and the Last Crusade, and again, in
1991, in *The Fisher King*.

REVIEWS

The picture is overdrawn and somewhat
tedious, but producer-director Victor Saville
still manages to instill interest in what's going
on, and even hits a feeling of excitement occasionally.

Variety

In spinning the saga of the cup from which
Christ drank at the Last Supper, they have
employed a largely tested cast that rarely dis-
tills emotion or appreciable conviction from
their roles . . . . Though it is lavish and sweeping in execution, *The Silver Chalice*, for all its
august and religious aspects, is not an impos-
ing offering.

New York Times

DAY OF TRIUMPH

1954 Century Films

CREDITS

Directors: Irving Pichel, John T. Coyle; *Producer:*
James K. Friedrich; *Screenplay:* Arthur T. Horman;
Photography (Eastmancolor): Ray June; *Music:* Daniele
Amfitheatrof; *Film Editor:* Thomas Neff. *Running
Time:* 110 minutes.

CAST

Robert Wilson played *Jesus* in a cast that included:
Lee J. Cobb (*Zadok*); Ralph Freud (*Caiaphas*); Tyler
McVey (*Peter*); Touch Connors (*Andrew*); Tony
Gerry (*Cloas*); Joanne Dru (*Mary Magdalene*), James
Griffith (*Judas*), Everett Glass (*Annas*); Lowell Gil-
more (*Pontius Pilate*); Anthony Warde (*Barabbas*);
Peter Whitney (*Nikator*); WITH John Stevenson.

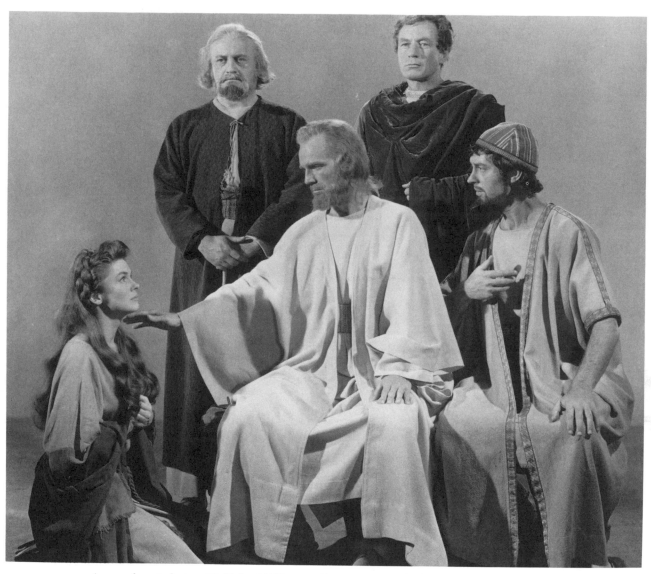

DAY OF TRIUMPH: A posed cast shot, with Robert Wilson as Jesus, surrounded by Joanne Dru (Mary Magdalene), Lee J. Cobb (Zadok), Lowell Gilmore (Pilate), and James Griffith (Judas).

COMMENTARY

Rev. James K. Friedrich, head of Cathedral Films which produced nontheatrical motion pictures for church and classroom, released his most ambitious effort to theaters in 1954. *Day of Triumph,* distributed by Century Films, starred Robert Wilson, who had played Jesus in Cathedral's *I Beheld His Glory* as well as in sound filmstrips produced by the company. (Veteran actor Lowell Gilmore also played Pilate in both films.) *Day of Triumph* featured a solid cast of well-known Hollywood performers such as Lee J. Cobb and Joanne Dru (as Mary Magdalene), and a young Touch (later to become Mike) Connors. The last film directed by Hollywood veteran Irving Pichel (with co-direction by John T. Coyle), *Day of Triumph* was filmed in California's Vasquez Rocks area at a cost of $600,000, and was enhanced with fine color cinematography by Ray June. Although he is a bit too mature to play Jesus, Robert Wilson's performance is excellent, and the actor's fine work was lauded by reviewers. *Day of Triumph* has been seldom screened in recent years, a pity since it is one of the more sincere pictures of its type, and is also noteworthy

DAY OF TRIUMPH: Joanne Dru as Mary Magdalene.

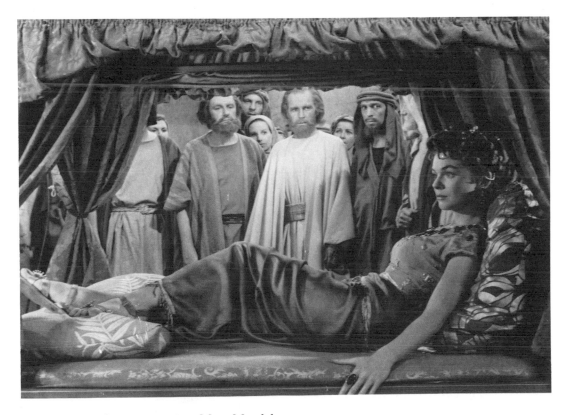

DAY OF TRIUMPH: Jesus encounters Mary Magdalene.

DAY OF TRIUMPH: Mary Magdalene at the feet of Jesus.

historically as the first American film dramatizing Christ's life since DeMille's 1927 silent *The King of Kings*.

REVIEW

A handsomely mounted independent production that abounds in dignity, restraint and distinction . . . . Most of the story has a documentary flavor and is without the familiar embellishments usually added to so-called biblical yarns in the interest of entertainment . . . Particularly well-done is Robert Wilson's portrayal of Christ. His humble, saintly and reverent interpretation comes close to duplicating the picture of Christ as seen through the Bible.

Variety

DAY OF TRIUMPH: Jesus meets with the Disciples.

DAY OF TRIUMPH: Robert Wilson (center).

DAY OF TRIUMPH: Jesus with Judas at the Last Supper.

DAY OF TRIUMPH: Jesus raises Lazarus from the dead.

DAY OF TRIUMPH: Jesus being betrayed by Judas at Gethsemane.

DAY OF TRIUMPH: Jesus on trial before Pilate.

DAY OF TRIUMPH: The Last Supper.

DAY OF TRIUMPH: Robert
Wilson (center) as Jesus.

102

THE PRODIGAL

1955 Metro-Goldwyn-Mayer

CREDITS

Director: Richard Thorpe; *Producer:* Charles Schnee; *Screenplay:* Maurice Zimm, Joe Breen, Jr., Samuel James Larsen; *Photography (CinemaScope, Eastmancolor):* Joseph Ruttenberg; *Music:* Bronislau Kaper; *Film Editor:* Harold F. Kress; *Art Directors:* Cedric Gibbons, Randall Duell; *Set Design:* Edwin B. Willis, Henry Grace; *Costumes:* Herschel McCoy; *Special Effects:* A. Arnold Gillespie, Warren Newcombe; *Makeup:* William Tuttle. *Running Time:* 114 minutes.

CAST

Lana Turner (*Samarra, High Priestess of Astarte*); Edmund Purdom (*Micah*); Louis Calhern (*Nahreeb, High Priest of Baal*); Audrey Dalton (*Ruth*); James Mitchell (*Asham*); Neville Brand (*Rhakim*); Walter Hampton (*Eli, Micah's Father*); Taina Elg (*Elissa*); Francis L. Sullivan (*Bosra, the Moneylender*); Joseph Wiseman (*Carmish*); Sandra Descher (*Yasmin*); John Dehner (*Joram*); Cecil Kellaway (*Governor*); Philip Tonge (*Barber/Surgeon*); Henry Daniell (*Ramadi*); Paul Cavanaugh (*Tobiah*); Dayton Lummis (*Caleb*); Tracey Roberts (*Tahra*); Jarma Lewis (*Uba*); Jay Novello (*Merchant*); Dorothy Adams (*Carpenter's Wife*); Peter DeBear (*Carpenter's Son*); Phyllis Graffeo (*Miriam*); Patricia Iannone (*Deborah*); Eugene Mazzola (*David*); George Sawaya (*Kavak*); Richard Devon (*Risafe*); Ann Cameron (*Lahla*); Gloria Dea (*Faradine*); John Rosser (*Lirhan*); Charles Wagenheim (*Zubeir*); Gordon Richards (*Scribe*); Paul Bryer (*Townsman*); Rex Lease (*Purveyor*); George Lewis (*Guard*); Almira Sessions (*Old Lady*); Chuck Roberson (*Chieftain*); Tom Steele (*Slave*); Goria Stone (*Mouse*); Linda Danson (*Owl*); Joanne Dale (*Bunny*); Lucille Maracini (*Ram*); Lila Zali (*Monkey*); Diane Gump (*Fox*);Patricia

THE PRODIGAL: Lana Turner.

THE PRODIGAL: Edmund Purdom and Lana Turner.

Jackson (*Lion*); John Damler (*Jailer*); Argentina Brunetti (*Woman*); Jo Gilbert (*Mother*); George Robotham (*Martyr*); David Leonard (*Blind Man*).

COMMENTARY

The New Testament parable of the Prodigal Son, related by Jesus over twenty-two verses in Luke XV, was initially filmed by Pathé in 1909. Subsequent versions included one from Eclair in 1911, followed by director Raoul Walsh's much more substantial 1925 Paramount silent, *The Wanderer*. The 1955 MGM version, *The Prodigal*, remains the most lavish treatment to date, relating the tale of Micah (Edmund Purdom), who squanders his family inheritance on the favors of a pagan temple priestess, Samarra (Lana Turner). In spite of her flaunting her wiles and her attempts to influence him with her evil pagan beliefs, Micah refuses to forsake God and rejects Samarra.

Like the previous *Salomé* with Rita Hayworth, *The Prodigal* was produced as a vehicle for a fading Hollywood sex symbol, in this case, Lana Turner. Since the film was a tailormade star vehicle, Turner is allowed to inter-

THE PRODIGAL: Francis L. Sullivan (reclining), Lana Turner, and Louis Calhern.

104

THE PRODIGAL: Louis Calhern, Edmund Purdom, and Lana Turner.

THE PRODIGAL: Bald Neville Brand and Edmund Purdom.

105

THE PRODIGAL: Lana Turner.

prct hcr potentially lurid role in a curiously innocent and sympathetic manner, to the extent that her climactic death by stoning (an ineffective scene in which Turner is unconvincingly pelted with foam rubber rocks before tumbling into a flaming pit) even seems undeserved! The nadir of this expensive spectacle was an unintentionally ludicrous scene in which leading man Purdom desperately fights an attacking vulture, portrayed by a stiff and lifeless rubber puppet. (This epic effectively ended Turner's status as queen of the MGM lot as well as Purdom's Hollywood sojourn.)

There are a couple of huge, well-designed, visually impressive sets, made even more striking by Joseph Ruttenberg's vibrant Technicolor photography, but Richard Thorpe's direction fails to bring any life to the picture. MGM attempted to entice audiences with a glossy promotional trailer that was nearly ten minutes long and promised a good deal more than the well-mounted but ultimately boring film delivered.

REVIEWS

Producer Charles Schnee has filled the picture so full of scene and spectacle that Richard Thorpe's direction is hard put to give it any semblance of movement, or to get life and warmth into the characters and incidents.

Variety

Take our advice and view it lightly—or as lightly as one can view a couple of million dollars worth of posturing in a long and old-fashioned pastiche of *Ben-Hur*. For this is not serious screen drama in the mature and modern sense of the phrase. This is romantic, pompous, ostentatious and often vulgar and ridiculous charade. . . . Miss Turner plays with the dignity and sense of high destiny you might expect of a heroine walking the last mile down a runway of Minsky's burlesque.

New York Times

CELUI QUI DOIT MOURIR
(He Who Must Die)
France / Italy
1956 Lopert

CREDITS

Director: Jules Dassin; *Producer:* Henri Berard; *Screenplay:* Ben Barzman, Jules Dassin (*based on the novel* Christ Recrucified *by* Nikos Kazantzakis); *Dialogue:* André Obey; *Photography* (*CinemaScope*): Jacques Natteau; *Music:* Georges Auric; *Film Editors:* Pierre Gillette, Roger Dwyre; *Art Director:* Max Douy. *Running Time:* 124 minutes.

CAST

Carl Mohner (*Lukas*); Roger Hanin (*Panayotaros*); Melina Mercouri (*Katerina*); Jean Servais (*Fotis*); Pierre Vaneck (*Manolis*); Gregoire Aslan (*Agha*); Gert Froebe (*Patriarcheas*); Teddy Bilis (*Hadji Nikolis*); Rene Lefevre (*Yannakos*); Lucien Raimbourg (*Kostandis*); Dimos Starenios (*Ladas*); Fernand Ledoux (*Popo Grigoris*); Maurice Ronet (*Michelis*); Nicole Berger (*Mariori*).

COMMENTARY

This French-made allegory by director Jules Dassin, filmed in Crete two years before its American release, was based on the novel *O Christos Xanastauronetai* (*Christ Recrucified*) by Nikos Kazantzakis, who also wrote the novel, *The Last Temptation of Christ*. The story takes place in a Greek village where the citizens are about to stage their annual Passion Play when a horde of starving war refugees descend on the town seeking shelter. The town council opposes charity for the refugees, but the cast of the Passion Play, especially Manolis (Pierre Vaneck), the young man chosen to portray Jesus, insists on helping the suffering people, who have camped on a nearby hill. The council remains inflexible, though, and in an emotionally wrenching scene, Manolis is murdered by the town leaders—stabbed to death by the man cast as Judas in the Passion Play. Expatriate American director Jules Dassin, ostracized from Hollywood because of his alleged left-wing sympathies, relocated in France and continued his career there in the 1950s. Dassin abased the visual aspects of *He Who Must Die*

HE WHO MUST DIE: Melina Mercouri and Peter Veneck.

on the classic films of Russian directors Eisenstein and Pudovkin; the impressive black-and-white photography is by Jacques Natteau, shooting on location. Although highly praised at the time of its release, *He Who Must Die* today is neglected and seldom seen.

REVIEWS

Director Dassin has not quite welded the two story aspects, and the development is uneven. The second half is full of action and revolt, thus taking on a more dynamic air but does not quite bring it off. Acting is somewhat theatrical and Pierre Vaneck rarely gets the dignity into the role of shepherd who becomes a liberator after he is picked to play the Christ part.

Variety

. . . Plainly has as its theme the horrible irony in the pretense of Christian virtue that some worldly people make. If Christ returned to earth today, these selfish people would still crucify him for his social teachings, this drama says.

New York Times

HE WHO MUST DIE

... A film of such rare, uncompromising honesty and uprightness that one longs to be completely won to it and to admire it frankly. Unfortunately, the longing is left unsatisfied. Perhaps the trouble is that the original novel, which, it is said, contains qualities of deep religious feeling and of philosophy, is just not the kind of material which can be readily conveyed through images.

Monthly Film Bulletin

IL MAESTRO
(The Teacher and the Miracle)
Italy/Spain

1957 Gladiator–Union

CREDITS

Producer/Director: Aldo Fabrizi (*U. S. version directed by* Carol Risthof, Peter Riethof); *Screenplay:* Aldo Fabrizi, L. Lucas, J. Gallardo, Mario Amendola; *Photography:* Antonio Macasoli, Manuel Merino; *Music:* Carlo Innocenzi. *Running Time:* 88 minutes.

CAST

Aldo Fabrizi (*Giovanni Merino*); Eduardo Nevola (*Antonio*); Marco Paoletti (*Gabriel*); Alfredo Mayo (*Principal*); Mary Lamar (*Teacher*); Felix Fernandez (*Porter*); Julio San Juan (*Doctor*); José Calvo (*Chauffeur*); Julia Caba Alba (*Portress*).

COMMENTARY

An Italian-Spanish coproduction, produced, directed, and cowritten by Aldo Fabrizi, who also starred, this film told the story of an aging, widowed school instructor who, dispirited over the death of his son in a car accident, loses his faith and enthusiasm for life. He begins to enjoy teaching again, his enthusiasm renewed by the arrival of a bright new student, Gabriel (Marco Paoletti), in his class, but is puzzled when Gabriel suddenly disappears. Searching for the youngster, he enters a church where he sees a sculpture of the Madonna and Child, the Christ Child bearing the exact features of the missing student. This simple and understated allegory was marred somewhat when twelve

minutes of its original one-hundred-minute running time were cut for the American release in 1961.

REVIEW

It's a sad fact that a spiritual theme doesn't necessarily mean a good picture. . . . The plot, in steady hands, might have provided a quietly inspirational little film, particularly had it relied on the power of suggestion. The release is unquestionably wholesome, tender and straightforward. It also happens to be as slow as molasses and twice as sticky.

New York Times

ORDET (The Word)
Denmark

1957 Palladium/Kingsley International

CREDITS

Producer/Director/Screenplay: Carl Theodor Dreyer (*based on the play by* Kaj Munk); *Photography:* Henning Bendtsen; *Film Editor:* Edith Schussel; *Music:* Poul Schierbeck; *Art Direction:* Erik Aaes. *Running Time:* 126 minutes.

CAST

Henrik Malberg (*Morten Borgen*); Emil Hass Christensen (*Mikkel Borgen*); Preben Lerdoff-Rye (*Johannes Borgen*); Cay Christensen (*Anders Borgen*); Brigitte Federspiel (*Inger, Mikkel's Wife*); Ejner Federspiel (*Peter Skraedder*); Ove Rud (*Pastor*); Ann Elisabeth Rud (*Maren Borgen, Mikkel's Daughter*); Susanne Rud (*Lilleinger Borgen, Mikkel's Daughter*); Gerda Nielsen (*Anne Skraedder*); Sylvia Eckhausen (*Kirstine Skraedder*); Henry Skjaer (*Doctor*); Hanne Agesen (*Karen, a Servant*); Edith Thrane (*Mette Maren*).

COMMENTARY

Made in 1955 but not released in America until two years later, respected director Carl Theodor Dreyer's Danish film is an incisive allegory about a man (Henrik Malberg) whose son (Preben Lerdoff-Rye) believes himself to be Jesus Christ. He is considered insane until he is

THE TEACHER AND THE MIRACLE: Marco Paoletti as the Christ Child.

ORDET: From left: Cay Christensen, Henrik Malberg, Ejner Federspiel, Gerda Nielsen, and Sylvia Eckhausen.

visited by the Holy Spirit and raises his brother's wife from the dead.

Dreyer strips the film down to bare essentials (it is constructed of only 114 separate shots in the entire 126 minutes), resulting in a funereal pace that supports the picture's meditative and religious qualities. Composer Poul Schierbeck, slated to compose the score for *Ordet*, died before completing work on the film, and Dreyer found several of the compositions among Schierbeck's papers, and used them for the picture. Playwright Kaj Munk, on whose work this film was based, was also a clergyman. Widely known in Scandinavia, Munk was tragically murdered by the Nazis during their occupation, his body discovered in a roadside ditch. *Ordet* is a fitting memorial, an intellectual meditation on the nature of faith. Shot with hypnotic conviction, the film was universally hailed as a masterpiece by critics.

REVIEWS

Acting is perfect as is the direction, which

ORDET: Gerda Nielsen.

ORDET: From left: Ove Rud, Brigitte Federspiel, Emil Hass Christensen, Henrik Malberg, and Cay Christensen.

makes this a profound study of faith and belief.

Variety

A visual sermon of scalding, spiritual intensity, it uncoils, when it moves at all, like a majestic snail.

New York Times

THE BIG FISHERMAN

1959 Buena Vista

CREDITS

Director: Frank Borzage; *Producer:* Rowland V. Lee; *Screenplay:* Howard Eastabrook, Rowland V. Lee (*based on the novel by* Lloyd C. Douglas); *Photography (70mm, Eastmancolor):* Lee Garmes; *Music:* Albert Hay Malotte; *Film Editor:* Paul Weatherwax; *Production Design:* John DeCuir; *Set Decoration:* Julia Heron; *Costumes:* Renie. *Running Time:* 180 minutes.

THE BIG FISHERMAN: Herbert Lom as Herod Antipas, Martha Hyer as Herodias.

CAST

Howard Keel (*Simon Peter*); Susan Kohner (*Fara*); John Saxon (*Voldi*); Martha Hyer (*Herodias*); Herbert Lom (*Herod Antipas*); Ray Stricklyn (*Deran*); Marian Seldes (*Amon*); Alexander Scourby (*David Ben-Za-dok*); Beulah Bondi (*Hannah*); Jay Barney (*John the Baptist*); Charlotte Fletcher (*Rennah*); Mark Dana (*Zendi*); Rhodes Reason (*Andrew*); Henry Brandon (*Menicus*); Brian Hutton (*John*); Thomas Troupe (*James*); Marianne Stewart (*Ione*); Jonathan Harris (*Lysias*); Leonard Mudie (*Ilderan*); James Griffith (*The Beggar*); Peter Adams (*Herod-Phillip*); Jo Gilbert (*Deborah*); Michael Mark (*Innkeeper*); Joe Di Reda (*Arab Assassin*); Stuart Randall (*King Aretas*); Herbert Rudley (*Emperor Tiberius*); Phillip Fine (*Lucius*); Francis McDonald (*Scribe Spokesman*); Perry Ivins (*Pharisee Spokesman*); Ralph Moody (*Aged Pharisee*); Tony Jochim (*Sadducee Spokesman*); Dan Turner (*Roman Captain*).

COMMENTARY

Rev. James K. Friedrich's Centurion Films produced *The Big Fisherman* for distribution by Walt Disney's Buena Vista company.

THE BIG FISHERMAN: Howard Keel as Simon Peter.

Filmed in 70mm Eastmancolor by veteran cinematographer Lee Garmes (who succeeded in making the San Fernando Valley look like Palestine) and directed by Frank Borzage, the story juxtaposed the life of Simon Peter (Howard Keel) with a love story between a prince and princess (John Saxon and Susan Kohner). Considering the technical finesse expected from Disney, there are surprising gaffes in the film, including microphone booms and klieg lights glimpsed in several scenes. At this time, the Disney organization was attempting to move away from its increasingly expensive animated cartoon features toward family-oriented live-action pictures (and with a large degree of success), but this ill-advised venture, in which the most dramatic story of all time is used as mere support for a contrived romance, was definitely a misstep for the studio. Jesus Christ is shown with even more restraint than usual, His presence indicated by an extended off-screen hand or the dangling hem of a robe,

116

THE BIG FISHERMAN: Howard Keel and an off-screen Jesus.

THE BIG FISHERMAN: Howard Keel, with Susan Kohner (left) and Beulah Bondi.

with an anonymous voice dubbed over the scenes.

REVIEWS

A pious but plodding account of the conversion to Christianity of Simon Peter, the Apostle called "the fisher of men." Its treatment is reverent but so far from rousing that in its present three-hour running time it is far overlength.

Variety

Honestly reverential but rarely moving. As a three-hour illustration of potentially memorable events surrounding the origins of Christianity, it is largely majestic, plodding and pictorial rather than persuasive drama.

New York Times

BEN-HUR

1959 Metro-Goldwyn-Mayer

CREDITS

Director: William Wyler; *Producer:* Sam Zimbalist; *Screenplay:* Karl Tunberg (*based on the novel by* Lew Wallace); *Photography* (*Camera 65, Panavision, Technicolor*): Robert L. Surtees; *Music:* Miklos Rozsa; *Film Editors:* Ralph E. Winters, John Dunning; *Art Directors:* William Horning, Edward Carfagno; *Costumes:* Elizabeth Haffenden; *Special Effects:* A. Arnold Gillespie, Robert MacDonald; *Assistant Directors:* Andrew Marton, Yakima Canutt, Mario Soldati. *Running Time:* 212 minutes.

CAST

Claude Heater played *Jesus* in a cast that included: Charlton Heston (*Judah Ben-Hur*); Jack Hawkins (*Quintus Arrius*); Stephen Boyd (*Messala*); Haya Harareet (*Esther*); Hugh Griffith (*Sheik Ilderim*); Martha Scott (*Miriam*); Sam Jaffe (*Simonides*); Cathy O'Donnell (*Tirzah*); Finlay Currie (*Balthasar*); Frank Thring (*Pontius Pilate*); Terence Longden (*Drusus*); André Morell (*Sextus*); Marina Berti (*Flavia*); George Ralph (*Tiberius*); Adi Berber (*Malluch*); Stella Vitelleschi (*Amrah*); Jose Greci (*Mary*); Laurence Payne (*Joseph*); John Horsley (*Spintho*); Richard Coleman (*Metellus*); Duncan Lamont (*Marius*); Ralph Truman

(*Aide to Tiberius*); Richard Hale (*Gaspar*); Reginald La Singh (*Melchior*); David Davies (*Quaestor*); Dervis Ward (*Jailer*); Mino Doro (*Gratus*); Robert Brown (*Chief of Rowers*); John Glenn (*Rower #42*); Maxwell Shaw (*Rower #43*); Emile Carrer (*Rower #28*); Tutte Lemkow (*Leper*); Howard Lang (*Hortator*); Ferdy Mayne (*Captain of Rescue Ship*); John Le Mesurier (*Doctor*); Stevenson Lang (*Blind Man*); Aldo Mozele (*Barca*); Thomas O'Leary (*Starter at Race*); Noel Sheldon (*Centurion*); Hector Ross (*Officer*); Bill Kuehl (*Soldier*); Aldo Silvani (*Man in Nazareth*); Diego Pozzetto (*Villager*); Dino Fazio (*Morcello*); Michael Cosmo (*Raimondo*); Aldo Pial (*Cavalry Officer*); Remington Olmstead (*Decurion*); Victor De La Fosse (*Galley Officer*); Enzio Fiermonte (*Galley Officer*); Hugh Billingsley (*Mario*); Tiberio Mitri (*Roman at Bath*); Pietro Tordi (*Pilate's Servant*); Jerry Brown (*The Corinthian*); Otello Capanna (*The Byzantine*); Luigi Marra (*Syrian*); Cliff Lyons (*Lubian*); Edward J. Auregal (*Athenian*); Joe Yrigoyan (*Egyptiun*); Alfredo Danesi (*Armenian*); Raimondo Van Riel (*Old Man*); Mike Dugan (*Seaman*); Joe Canutt (*Sportsman*).

COMMENTARY

MGM's 1959 remake of *Ben-Hur* was the ultimate 1950s religious spectacle. The mammoth production, running three hours and thirty-two minutes (with a fifteen-minute intermission in the original theatrical presentation) was a considerable gamble for the studio, in dire financial straits at the time. Directed by William Wyler at a then-staggering cost of $12.5 million, filmed in 65mm Technicolor on three hundred sets sprawling across more than three-hundred-forty acres (the arena for the chariot race alone covered eighteen acres) and with more than eight thousand extras for the crowd scenes, *Ben-Hur*, there can be no denying, is physically and visually impressive. The film has an unusually intelligent screenplay (credited to Karl Tunberg, with uncredited contributions from Maxwell Anderson, S. N. Behrman, Gore Vidal, and Christopher Fry), and yet something much more essential is missing; the movie simply lacks the heart of the 1925 original, and falls short of the earlier one in other ways as well.

The Nativity scenes in the 1959 movie are static, picture-postcard visuals, and are simply not as moving as the same sequence in the 1925 movie. The special effects in the 1959 version (by A. Arnold Gillespie and Robert MacDonald) are also surprisingly inferior, particularly the unconvincing sea battle, which was shot with obvious miniatures in a studio tank, whereas the silent film used full-scale ships. On the other hand, the 1959 picture does improve on its predecessor in a couple of instances; the acting is generally more controlled and subtle, and the scenes with Jesus Christ (played by Claude Heater in the remake) are less forced and contrived. The famous chariot race, although exciting and spectacular in the silent version, was marred by camera undercranking that produced fast-speed action too frantic and stylized; the same scene in the remake, directed by action specialists Andrew Marton and Yakima Canutt, is riveting and more impressive. For the 1959 chariot race, 40,000 tons of sand were transported from beaches to cover the arena track, and it took one year for more than a thousand workers to construct the huge arena set. Before actual filming of the sequence began, Stephen Boyd and Charlton Heston both received extensive training and careful rehearsal from supervising stuntman Canutt.

BEN-HUR (1959): Charlton Heston, as Judah Ben-Hur, his thirst quenched by the helping hand of Jesus.

BEN-HUR (1959): The Nativity.

BEN-HUR 1959): Jesus stands before Pilate (Frank Thring).

120

BEN-HUR (1959): Messala (Stephen Boyd, left) and Ben-Hur (Charlton Heston) in the famed chariot race.

BEN-HUR (1959): Jesus (Claude Heater) speaks to his followers.

121

(OVERLEAF) BEN-HUR (1959): The Crucifixion.

BEN-HUR (1959): Charlton Heston, Cathy O'Donnell, and Martha Scott.

About equally balanced in its flaws and virtues, the 1959 *Ben-Hur*, which sprang to life onscreen from over 15,000 production sketches, was also a fitting epitaph for producer Sam Zimbalist, who suffered a fatal heart attack during production. The picture was an immense success, ultimately enriching Metro

124

to the tune of $40 million and garnering an unprecedented eleven Academy Awards.

REVIEWS

The big difference between *Ben-Hur* and other spectacles, biblical or otherwise, is its sincere concern for human beings. They're not just pawns reciting flowery dialogue to fill gaps between the action and spectacle scenes. They arouse genuine emotional feeling in the audience. . . . That the story is never trite or corny, factors that have detracted from previous biblical films, is a tribute to the script and director William Wyler.

Variety

Metro-Goldwyn-Mayer and William Wyler

have managed to engineer a remarkably intelligent and engrossing human drama in their new production of *Ben-Hur*. . . . Their mammoth color movie . . . is by far the most stirring and respectable of the Bible-fiction pictures ever made. . . . The artistic quality and taste of Mr. Wyler have prevailed to make this a rich and glowing drama that far transcends the bounds of spectacle.

New York Times

Great credit goes to producer Zimbalist, scenarist Tunberg and director Wyler, but the greatest belongs to Wyler. His wit, intelligence and formal instinct are almost everywhere in evidence, and he has set a standard of excel-

BEN-HUR (1959): Jesus (Claude Heater) bearing his cross to Calvary.

BEN-HUR (1959): The Crucifixion.

lence by which coming generations of screen spectacles can expect to be measured.

Time

DESERT DESPERADOES

(aka The Sinner)

1959 RKO

CREDITS

Director: Steve Sekely; *Producer:* John Nasht; *Screenplay:* Victor Stoloff, Robert Hill (*based on a story by* Stoloff and Hill); *Photography:* Massimo Dallamano. *Running Time:* 81 minutes.

CAST

Ruth Roman (*The Woman*); Akim Tamiroff (*The Merchant*); Othelo Toso (*Verrus*); Gianni Glori (*Fabius*); Arnoldo Foa (*The Chaldean*); Alan Furlan (*Rais*); Nino Marchetti (*Metullus*).

COMMENTARY

Desert Desperadoes, also known under an alternate title, *Flight Into Egypt,* was a minor but offbeat biblical action film, starring Ruth Roman as a woman stranded, in the desert, who is discovered by wealthy merchant Akim Tamiroff's caravan. Here the story takes an allegorical turn as it is inferred that a baby carried on the journey may be the infant Jesus. Released in the last days of RKO as a production/distribution entity, this low-budget film benefited from location shooting in Italy and Egypt, and was English-dubbed for American distribution. Ruth Roman, a popular leading lady of the early fifties, appeared here in one of her last top-billed roles before settling into character parts.

REVIEW

A meller of the old-fashioned cinema school set in biblical times. The theatrical values are limited. . .

Variety

MORE FILMS OF THE 1950s

The Fallen Star (NDF Distributors, 1951) was a pretentious West German feature with Jesus Christ and Satan battling over the soul of a

DESERT DESPERADOES: Akim Tamiroff (center).

woman. Directed by Harald Braun from a screenplay he cowrote with Herbert Witt, the picture collapsed under the weight of unnecessarily dense symbolism.

Il Cristo Pribito (*The Forbidden Christ*) (Excelsa, 1951), an Italian allegory, has a World War II veteran (Raf Vallone) returning to a small village in search of the traitor who had betrayed his partisan brother to the Nazis. Swearing to avenge his brother's death, he finds that none of the villagers, tired of bloodshed, will name the traitor. Finally, a guilt-ridden man, who had committed murder years before, decides to sacrifice himself in order to end the violence and tricks the war veteran into believing that it was he who betrayed his brother. The veteran mortally wounds him, but as he dies the man reveals the truth, pleading for an end to further violence. Well-directed by Curzio Malaparte, *The Forbidden Christ* also benefitted from elegant black-and-white photography by Gabor Pogani.

A non-theatrical film of the period is also deserving of mention. *The Westminster Passion Play—Behold the Man* (Film Reports/Companions of the Cross, 1951) was a seventy-five-

DESERT DESPERADOES: Ruth Roman (center).

127

minute British church production based on the Walter Meyjes and Charles P. Carr play *Ecce Homo*. Carr also played Jesus in the film, which was distributed by Universal in Great Britain.

Barabbas, the story (based on the novel by Par Lägervist) of a thief who is haunted by guilt when he is pardoned so that Jesus Christ may be crucified in his place, was first translated to the screen as a feature-length film in director Alf Sjöberg's little-known 1952 Swedish version, starring Ulf Palme in the title role. This interpretation would be completely overshadowed by the much more widely-seen Anthony Quinn version of 1962.

Marcelino (Chamartin) was a charming 1954 Spanish film by director Ladislao Vajda, released in America two years later, about the miracle that occurs in a monastery when a small boy, adopted by monks, speaks with

DESERT DESPERADOES: Akim Tamiroff (center).

DESERT DESPERADOES: Ruth Roman (center).

128

Jesus Christ when he offers a life-size crucifix figure bread and wine, bringing the effigy to life. In its October 22, 1956, review, the *New York Times* hailed the film as "one of those lovely little pictures that stand out oddly on the cold commercial screen, for it is, in its theme and essence, a very special religious fantasy."

The Power of the Resurrection (Family Films, 1958) was a non-theatrical feature, produced for church use and television showings, about the Apostle Peter (Richard Kiley), relating the last days of Jesus Christ (Jon Shepodd) to a young Christian persecuted for his beliefs. Directed by Harold Schuster, the one-hour feature was shot in color at Keywest Studios in Hollywood.

KING OF KINGS (1961): Joseph and Mary at the Nativity.

CHAPTER 6

THE NINETEEN SIXTIES

KING OF KINGS

1961 Metro-Goldwyn-Mayer

CREDITS

Director: Nicholas Ray; *Producer:* Samuel Bronston; *Screenplay:* Philip Yordan; *Photography (Technirama 70, Technicolor):* Franz F. Planer, Milton Krasner, Manuel Berenguer; *Narration Written by:* Ray Bradbury; *Music:* Miklos Rozsa; *Film Editors:* Harold Kress, Renee Lichtig; *Set Designer/Costumes:* George Wakhevitch; *Special Effects:* Alex C. Weldon, Lee LeBlanc; *Choreography:* Betty Utey; *Makeup:* Mario Van Riel, Charles Parker; *Associate Producers:* Alan Brown, Jaime Prades. *Running Time:* 168 minutes.

CAST

Jeffrey Hunter played *Jesus* in a cast that included: Siobhan McKenna (*Mary*); Hurd Hatfield (*Pontius Pilate*); Ron Randell (*Lucius, the Centurion*); Viveca Lindfors (*Claudia*); Rita Gam (*Herodias*); Carmen Sevilla (*Mary Magdalene*); Brigid Bazlen (*Salomé*); Harry Guardino (*Barabbas*); Rip Torn (*Judas*); Frank Thring (*Herod Antipas*); Guy Rolfe (*Caiaphas*); Maurice Marsac (*Nicodemus*); Gregoire Aslan (*King Herod*); Royal Dano (*Peter*); Edric Connor (*Balthazar*); Robert Ryan (*John the Baptist*); George Coulouris (*Camel Driver*); Conrado San Martin (*General Pompey*); Gerard Tichy (*Joseph*); José Antonio (*Young John*); Luis Prendes (*Good Thief*); David Davies (*Burly Man*); José Nieto (*Caspar*); Ruben Rojo (*Matthew*); Fernando Sancho (*Madman*); Michael Wager (*Thomas*); Felix de Pomes (*Joseph of Arimathea*); Adriano Rimoldi (*Melchior*); Barry Keegan (*Bad Thief*); Rafael Luis Calvo (*Simon of Cyrene*); Tino Barrero (*Andrew*); Francisco Moran (*Blind Man*); Orson Welles (*Narrator*).

COMMENTARY

MGM's 1961 production of *King of Kings* should have been the definitive cinematic life of Christ, but it falls somewhat short of that goal. Lavishly produced on a budget of $8 million and filmed in 70mm Technicolor on 396 sets over a period of four months, it is strangely uninvolving, largely due to the screenplay by Philip Yordan (with an uncredited assist from Ray Bradbury, who wrote the narration delivered by Orson Welles). Yordan's curious script, although neatly and precisely telescoping many of the events and pronouncements of

fine performances, the total effect is blunted by Yordan's counterproductive scripting, and the Roman Catholic Legion of Decency criticized the film as "theologically, historically, and scripturally inaccurate." Writing in *America*, a Jesuit weekly, reviewer Moira Walsh was particularly harsh in her critique: "There is not the slightest possibility that anyone will derive from the film any meaningful insight into what Christ's life and sufferings signify for us . . . . It is obvious that Bronston, Ray and Yordan have no opinion on the subject of Christ except that He is a hot box-office property."

Although partially justified, at least some of this adverse criticism was probably due to the fact that, by 1962, Hollywood's cycle of biblical

KING OF KINGS (1961): Jeffrey Hunter.

the Gospels, totally ignores a wealth of potentially dramatic material, such as Jesus's miracles, surely the most compelling work of his ministry. Only one miracle is shown, and a lesser one at that, as Jesus's shadow falls across a blind man and cures him. Yordan's screenplay also falls prey to conceited fictionalizing, inflating the role of Barabbas (hardly mentioned at all in the Bible) into that of a revolutionary leader, presenting two sprawling battles that never actually occurred, and even going so far as whitewashing Judas's motives for betraying Jesus, presenting him as merely a bewildered scapegoat.

Although the acting in *King of Kings* is generally excellent, with blue-eyed teen heartthrob Jeffrey Hunter (as Jesus), Harry Guardino (as Barabbas), Rip Torn (as Judas), and Siobhan McKenna (as the Virgin Mary) all delivering

132

films, launched at the beginning of the previous decade, was nearly played out. The public—and especially the critics—had simply been oversaturated with films of this type. Yordan's troubled script aside, *King of Kings* is a good film, perhaps not as well done as it might have been, but certainly better than many other religious pictures and undeserving of such hyperbolic criticism. Conceptually flawed yet undeniably sincere, *King of Kings* has stood the test of time rather well and seems better now than on its first release.

REVIEWS

Nicholas Ray has brooded long and wisely upon the meaning of his meanings, has

KING OF KINGS (1961): Siobhan McKenna as the Virgin Mary.

KING OF KINGS (1961): Gerard Tichy and Siobhan McKenna as Joseph and Mary, commanded to journey to Jerusalem to be counted and taxed.

KING OF KINGS (1961): Siobhan McKenna as Mary with the baby Jesus.

KING OF KINGS (1961): Jeffrey Hunter (white robe) as Jesus spies the wanton Mary Magdalene (Carmen Sevilla).

KING OF KINGS (1961): Jeffrey Hunter and Ron Randell (as Lucius, the Centurion).

KING OF KINGS (1961): Brigid Bazlen as a teenage Salomé, the siren who dances for the head of John the Baptist.

135

KING OF KINGS (1961): Frank Thring as Herod Antipas, the weakling puppet ruler of Judea.

KING OF KINGS (1961): Jesus at the Last Supper. Note the "Y"-shaped table, an inaccurate design unique to this version.

KING OF KINGS (1961): Peter (Royal Dano) looks on as Jesus offers a cup of wine to Matthew (Ruben Rojo) at the Last Supper.

KING OF KINGS (1961): Hurd Hatfield.

KING OF KINGS (1961): Robert Ryan (center) as John the Baptist and Brigid Bazlen as Salomé.

KING OF KINGS (1961): Hurd Hatfield (seated) as Pontius Pilate, with Ron Randell as Lucius, the Centurion.

KING OF KINGS (1961): Royal Dano as Peter, with Siobhan McKenna (Mary) and Carmen Sevilla (Mary Magdalene) listen to the Sermon on the Mount.

planted plenty of symbols along the path yet avoided the banalities of religious calendar art.

Variety

Of it all, let us say the spirit is hinted but the projection of it is weak.

New York Times

The definitive criticism of Bronston's Christ, and indeed of his entire film, is expressed in the snide subtitle by which it is widely known in the trade: "I Was a Teenage Jesus."

Time

WHISTLE DOWN THE WIND

Great Britain

1962 Rank (released in the U.S. by Walter Reade–Continental)

CREDITS

Director: Bryan Forbes; *Producer:* Richard Attenborough; *Screenplay:* Keith Waterhouse, Willis Hall

140

KING OF KINGS (1961): Jeffrey Hunter.

(based on the novel by Mary Hayley Bell); Photography: Arthur Ibbetson; *Music:* Malcolm Arnold; *Film Editor:* Max Benedict; *Art Director:* Ray Simm; *Makeup:* Geoffrey Rodway. *Running Time:* 98 minutes.

CAST

Hayley Mills (*Kathy Bostock*); Alan Bates (*Arthur Blakey, The Man*); Bernard Lee (*Mr. Bostock*); Diane Holgate (*Nan Bostock*); Alan Barnes (*Charles Bostock*); Norman Bird (*Eddie*); Diane Clare (*Miss Lodge*); Patricia Henegan (*Salvation Army Girl*); Elsie Wagstaff (*Auntie Dorothy*); John Arnatt (*Teesdale*); Hamilton Dyce (*Reeves*); Howard Douglas (*Weaver*); Roy Holder (*Jackie*); Gerald Sim (*Wilcox*); Ronald Hines (*Police Constable Thurstow*); Michael Lees, Michael Raghan (*Civil Defense Workers*); Barry Dean (*Raymond*); Mary Barton (*Villager*); Christine Ashworth,

KING OF KINGS (1961): Rip Torn as Judas, betraying Jesus.

KING OF KINGS (1961): Jesus sits unflinchingly while a crown of spiked thorns is placed on his head by Pompey (Conrado San Martin), one of Pilate's generals.

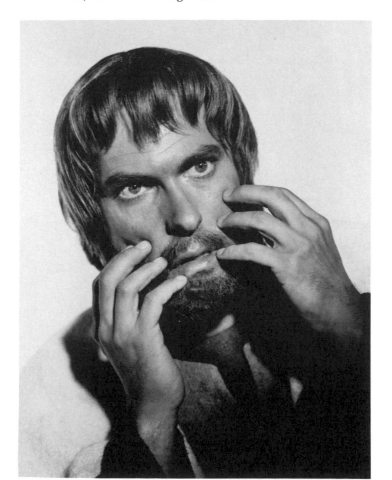

KING OF KINGS (1961): Rip Torn.

142

John Bodne, Doreena Clark, Keith Clement, Pamela Lonsdale, Judy Ollerneshaw, Robert Palmer, Lois Read, Nigel Stafford (*The Disciples*); Anne Newby, Julie Jackson (*The Latecomers*).

COMMENTARY

An allegorical drama from Great Britain, *Whistle Down the Wind* concerned an escaped convict (Alan Bates) who, hiding out in a country barn, is discovered by local children. When they ask who he is, the bearded figure cries out in desperate exhaustion, "Jesus Christ!" an exclamation taken literally by the children, who then proceed to secretly shelter and care for him. A charming, sensitive film that avoids mawkish contrivances, *Whistle Down the Wind*

KING OF KINGS (1961): Jesus bears the cross to Calvary.

WHISTLE DOWN THE WIND: Alan Bates as the stranger, discovered in a barn by Hayley Mills (light coat, top) and the children.

offers rare insight into the innocence and faith of children, and features excellent performances, especially that of Hayley Mills as one of the youngsters.

The author of the original novel, Mary Hayley Bell, was Hayley Mills's mother and actor John Mills's wife. *Whistle Down the Wind* was young Hayley's fourth movie.

REVIEWS

While it deals with sensitive material that might seem blasphemous to some—and indeed might well be embarrassing if it weren't handled with consummate skill and taste—it is beautifully simple, naturalistic and remote from religiosity as it tells, with great humor and compassion, of children and brotherly love.

New York Times

There are two themes here. One, an embarrassingly explicit allegory of Christ's portrayal, comes straight from Mary Hayley Bell's novel. The other is the film's own illustration of a childhood world, secret and fantastic and sufficiently sturdy to withstand the intrusion of a good deal of pretentious symbolism (the identification of the village children with the Disciples; the three betrayals with their echo of the apostle Peter).

Monthly Film Bulletin

BARABBAS

1962 Columbia

CREDITS

Director: Richard Fleischer; *Producer:* Dino De Laurentiis; *Screenplay:* Christopher Fry (*based on the novel by* Par Lagervist); *Photography* (*Technicolor, Technirama*): Aldo Tonti; *Music:* Mario Nascimbene; *Film Editor:* Raymond Poulton; *Art Director:* Mario Chiari; *Costumes:* Maria DeMatteis. *Running Time:* 144 minutes.

WHISTLE DOWN THE WIND: Hayley Mills and Alan Bates.

WHISTLE DOWN THE WIND: Alan Bates, arms outstretched against the skyline in the Christlike pose as seen by the children, while being searched by a detective (Gerald Sim) . . .

CAST

Roy Mangano played *Jesus* in a cast that included: Anthony Quinn (*Barabbas*); Silvana Mangano (*Rachel*); Arthur Kennedy (*Pontius Pilate*); Katy Jurado (*Sara*); Harry Andrews (*Peter*); Vittorio Gassman (*Sahak*); Jack Palance (*Torvald*); Ernest Borgnine (*Lucius*); Norman Wooland (*Rufio*); Valentina Cortese (*Julia*); Michael Gwynn (*Lazarus*); Douglas Fowley (*Vasasio*); Robert Hall (*Gladiator Captain*); Lawrence Payne (*Disciple*); Arnold Foa (*Joseph of Arimathea*); Ivan Triesault (*Emperor*); Joe Robinson (*Gladiator*); Guido Celano (*Scorpio*); Spartaco Nale (*Overseer*); Enrico Glori (*Important Gentleman*); Carlo Giustini, Frederich Ledebur, Gianni De Benedetto (*Officers*); Rina Braido (*Tavern Reveler*); Tullio Tomadoni (*Blind Man*); Maria Zanoli (*Beggar Woman*).

COMMENTARY

This was the second and most famous picture based on the Par Lagervist novel. Heading

a stellar cast is Anthony Quinn as the thief released from prison when Christ (played by Roy Mangano) is crucified in his place. The sumptuous Italian color production is graced with an incisive, thoughtful script by Christopher Fry. The story follows an initially unrepentant Barabbas as he first scorns Jesus's memory and then, eroded by his own experience as a gladiator and slave laborer, slowly

WHISTLE DOWN THE WIND: . . . and then led away by the authorities.

begins to comprehend why Jesus died and what His Crucifixion means. The story ends with Barabbas finally redeemed by his own crucifixion.

As the eternally suffering Barabbas, Quinn gives a sincere performance and plays every scene for all it is worth; his portrayal here is surely one of the most sweat-drenched in film history. Roy Mangano, who appears briefly as Jesus, was the brother of leading lady Silvana Mangano and was producer Dino De Laurentiis's brother-in-law. Arthur Kennedy, an excellent and shamefully underrated actor, provides effective support as Pontius Pilate, as does Jack Palance in the role of a sadistic gladiator. Also memorable are costars Katy Jurado and Ernest Borgnine, who were married at the time.

The film's production values were outstanding. Cinematographer Aldo Tonti's Technicolor lensing brought the required scope to the film's more spectacular scenes (particularly those occurring in an exploding sulphur mine), and Mario Nascimbene's vivid score enhanced the dramatics. Unfortunately, despite its genuine religious feeling, this particularly well-made film impressed many moviegoers as just another sword-and-sandal epic.

BARABBAS: Barabbas the gladiator.

BARABBAS: The Crucifixion.

BARABBAS: Barabbas on trial.

BARABBAS: Barabbas (Anthony Quinn) and prison mate Jesus Christ (Roy Mangano).

148

BARABBAS: Jesus is led off to Calvary as a confused Barabbas (center) looks on.

REVIEWS

Technically a fine job of work, reflecting big thinking and infinite patience on the parts of producer Dino De Laurentiis and director Richard Fleischer . . . . Where the film hits the bell is in Fleischer's bold, dramatic handling of certain scenes, allied to some slick lensing by Aldo Tonti.

Variety

Mr. Quinn is a sensational sufferer. He grunts and sweats and strains with more cred-ible vengeance and exertion than any actor we can name.

New York Times

The film is continuously alive, and what keeps it alive is the burning sincerity of its search for the reality of God and the meaning of the hero's singular and apocalyptic life.

Time

Barabbas marks the acme in the cinema's equation of Christianity with unrelieved mor-

149

BARABBAS: Barabbas (center) mock Jesus' Crucifixion.

BARABBAS: Vittorio Gassman (left), Ernest Borgnine, and Anthony Quinn.

BARABBAS: Barabbas (center) mocks Jesus's Crucifixion.

BARABBAS: Barabbas trains for combat in the arena.

BARABBAS: Silvana Mangano as Rachel, about to be stoned by the mob.

BARABBAS: Barabbas begging for forgiveness.

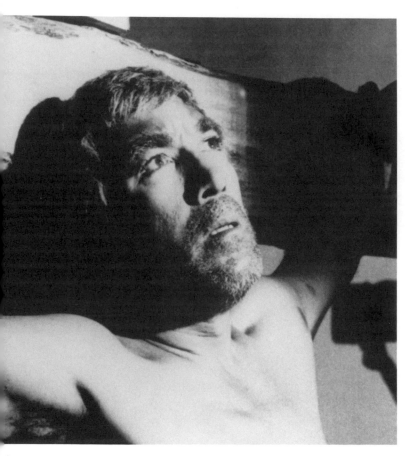

BARABBAS: The Crucifixion of Barabbas.

bidity. Opening with the scourge of Christ behind the credits, the depressing chronicle plods on through a stoning, the sulphur mines, gladitorial instruction and butchery, death by arrow, lion and cross to what is possibly the least uplifting ending yet achieved in the current and apparently endless cycle of biblical films . . . [It] remains throughout unacceptable in its pain-preoccupation and its religiosity.

Monthly Film Bulletin

PONZIO PILATO (Pontius Pilate)

Italy/France

1964 Glomer/Lux

CREDITS

Directors: Irving Rapper, Gian Paolo Callegari; *Exec-*

utive *Producer:* Enzo Merolle; *Screenplay:* Gino De Sanctis, O. Biancolo (*story by Gino De Sanctis*); *Photography* (*CinemaScope, Technicolor*): Massimo Dallamano; *Music:* A. F. Lavagnino; *Music Director:* Pierluigi Urbini. *Running time:* 100 minutes.

CAST

John Drew Barrymore played *Jesus* (as well as *Judas*) in a cast that included: Jean Marais (*Pontius Pilate*); Jeanne Crain (*Claudia Procula*); Basil Rathbone (*Caiphas*); Massimo Serato (*Nicodemus*); Riccardo Garrone (*Galba*); Livio Lorenzon (*Barabbas*); Gianni Garko (*Jonathon*); WITH Roger Treville, Carlo Giustini, Dante Di Paolo, Paul Muller, Alfredo Varelli, Manoela Ballard, Emma Baron, Raffaella Carra.

COMMENTARY

Filmed in 1961 under the title *Ponzio Pilato*, but not released in Europe until 1964 and lacking an American distributor until 1967, *Pontius Pilate* was an Italian-French coproduction telling the story of Christ's last days from the viewpoint of the title procurator (Jean Marais). In this film, thanks to a notable bit of publicity stunt casting, *both* Jesus Christ and Judas Iscariot are played (not very well) by the same actor, John Drew Barrymore. Although otherwise unremarkable, *Pontius Pilate* does feature an excellent performance by Basil Rathbone as Caiaphas, the chief rabbi of the Temple in Caesarea, who plots against Jesus because he fears the Saviour's growing popularity as a threat to his own power. Rathbone himself had been cast as Pilate years earlier in the previously described *The Last Days of Pompeii* (RKO, 1935), and significantly, Jean Marais's interpretation of Pilate in this movie falls short of Rathbone's. The female lead (as Pilate's wife, Claudia) was played by American actress Jeanne Crain in one of her last screen roles to date. Sparsely distributed and hardly reviewed at all, *Pontius Pilate* was unsuccessful in its limited theatrical release.

REVIEWS

A rambling screenplay, Irving Rapper's lethargic direction, poor dubbing, and, for the most part, uninteresting performances, detracted from what could have been a fascinat-

PONTIUS PILATE: John Drew Barrymore (extreme left) as Jesus.

153

PONTIUS PILATE: John Drew Barrymore (foreground) as Jesus.

PONTIUS PILATE: Jeanne Crain and John Drew Barrymore.

ing character study of the man who sent Christ to the Cross.

Michael Druxman, *Basil Rathbone: His Life and Films*

. . . Barrymore, in probably the most bizarre piece of gimmick casting ever seen, plays both Jesus and Judas, both of them badly. Nothing here that Cecil B. DeMille didn't do a hundred times better.

Motion Picture Guide

THE GREATEST STORY EVER TOLD

1965 United Artists

CREDITS

Producer/Director: George Stevens; *Screenplay:* George Stevens, James Lee Barrett (*based on* The

PONTIUS PILATE: Jean Marais (left) and Basil Rathbone (right).

THE GREATEST STORY EVER TOLD: Max Von Sydow as Jesus.

Bible, *the book by* Fulton Oursler, *and radio scripts by* Henry Denker); *Photography (Ultra-Panavision 70, Cinerama, Technicolor):* William C. Mellor, Loyal Griggs; *Music:* Alfred Newman; *Film Editors:* Harold F. Kress, Argyle Nelson, Jr., Frank O'Neill; *Art Directors:* Richard Day, William Creber, David Hall; *Set Designer:* David Hall; *Special Effects:* J. McMillan Johnson, Clarence Slifer, A. Arnold Gillespie, Robert Hoag; *Costumes:* Vittorio Nino Novarese, Marjorie Best. *Running Time:* 191 minutes.

CAST

Max Von Sydow played *Jesus* in a cast that included: Dorothy McGuire (*Mary*); Robert Loggia (*Joseph*); Claude Rains (*Herod the Great*); José Ferrer (*Herod Antipas*); Marian Seldes (*Herodias*); John Abbott (*Aben*); Rodolfo Acosta (*Captain of Lancers*); Philip Coolidge (*Chuza*); Michael Ansara (*Herod's Commander*); Dal Jenkins (*Philip*); Joe Perry (*Archelaus*); Charlton Heston (*John the Baptist*); Donald Pleasence (*The Dark Hermit*); David McCallum (*Judas Iscariot*); Roddy McDowall (*Matthew*); Michael Anderson, Jr. (*James the Younger*); David Sheiner (*James the Elder*); Gary Raymond (*Peter*); Robert Blake (*Simon the Zealot*); Burt Brinckerhoff (*Andrew*); John Considine (*John*); Jamie Farr (*Thaddaeus*); David Hedison (*Philip*); Peter Mann (*Nathaniel*); Tom Reese (*Thomas*); Telly Savalas (*Pontius Pilate*); Angela Lansbury (*Claudia*); Johnny Seven (*Pilate's Aide*); Paul Stewart (*Questor*); Harold J. Stone (*General Varus*); Cyril Delavanti (*Melchior*); Mark Leonard (*Balthazar*); Frank Silvera (*Caspar*); Joanna Dunham (*Mary Magdalene*); Janet Margolin (*Mary of Bethany*); Ina Balin (*Martha of Bethany*); Michael Tolan (*Lazarus*); Carroll Baker (*Veronica*); Pat Boone (*Man at Tomb*); Sal Mineo (*Uriah*); Van Heflin (*Bar Armand*); Ed Wynn (*Old Aram*); Shelley Winters (*Woman of No Name*); Chet Stratton (*Theophillus*); Ron Whelan (*Annas*); John Lupton (*Speaker of Capernaum*); Russell Johnson (*Scribe*); Abraham Sofaer (*Joseph of Arimathaea*); Martin Landau (*Caiaphas*); Nehemiah Persoff (*Shemiah*); Joseph Schildkraut (*Nicodemus*); Victor Buono (*Sorak*); Robert Busch (*Emissary*); John Crawford (*Alexander*); John Wayne (*Roman Captain*); Sidney Poitier (*Simon of Cyrene*); Richard Conte (*Barabbas*); Frank De Kova (*Tormentor*); Joseph Sirola (*Dumah*); John Pickard (*Peter's Second Accuser*); Celia Lovsky (*Woman Behind Railings*); Mickey Simpson (*Rabble Rouser*); Richard Bakalyan (*Good Thief on Cross*); Marc Cavell (*Bad Thief on Cross*); Renata Vanni (*Weeping Woman*).

THE GREATEST STORY EVER TOLD: Jesus on trial.

THE GREATEST STORY EVER TOLD: Carroll Baker and Max Von Sydow.

COMMENTARY

Filmed in Ultra-Panavision 70 and Technicolor at a cost of $20 million, *The Greatest Story Ever Told* is the pinnacle of Hollywood biblical epics and the most expensive life of Christ ever filmed.

When 20th Century-Fox had originally paid $100,000 for the rights to the best-selling 1949 book by Fulton Oursler (who had also, with Henry Denker, adapted the Bible to radio), Fox staff writer Philip Dunne (who had scripted

The Robe, David and Bathsheba and *Demetrius and the Gladiators*) declined the assignment. The project was then turned over to George Stevens and United Artists, with Stevens re-

ceiving a $1 million fee to produce, direct, and cowrite (with James Lee Barrett).

A solid, methodical director, Stevens had one basic flaw that hampered many of his films: an obsession with perfection. This is apparent, to varying degrees, even in his earliest work, and his constant, well-intentioned, but sometimes misguided striving for what he saw as quality either drove him stubbornly to include scenes that just did not work (as in the forced endings to both *Alice Adams* and *Swing Time*), or to shoot scenes until he had bled all the life and spontaneity from the material with multiple takes (as in *Shane*). This unfortunate trend reached its zenith in *The Greatest Story Ever Told*, but even though Stevens's direction is enervating, and the film's pacing suffers badly as a result, there is still much to admire visually, especially the precisely-framed compositions of the sweeping, rugged vistas shot on location in Utah and Arizona.

Handicapping the film more than the flawed direction was Stevens's unfortunate decision to insure box-office success by loading the picture with "guest stars" (Roddy McDowall, Ed Wynn, Angela Lansbury, Shelley Winters, Sidney Poitier, John Wayne, etc.); the effect is unintentionally devastating, almost totally crippling the film's believability.

Besides the wonderful photography, what really saves the movie from ruin are the otherwise fine performances in key roles: Max Von Sydow in a narrow but powerful interpretation of Jesus, Dorothy McGuire as the Virgin Mary, and Claude Rains as King Herod. Although restricted by the script's conception of Jesus, Von Sydow is quite good, and his portrayal of Christ ranks among the screen's best.

The Greatest Story Ever Told was originally released at a running time of four hours and twenty minutes; after disappointing box-office returns it was recut to three hours and fifty-eight minutes, then to three hours and seventeen minutes, and finally to three hours and ten minutes.

REVIEWS

Most distracting are the frequent pop-ups of familiar faces in so-called cameo roles, jarring the illusion of the moment with the diversion of the mind to the business of discovery.

New York Times

THE GREATEST STORY EVER TOLD: Max Von Sydow (foreground).

161

The sum of its merits is impressive. The residue of its defects is unimportant.

Variety

Stevens has outdone himself by producing an austere Christian epic that offers few excitements of any kind.

Time

IL VANGELO SECONDO MATTEO
(The Gospel According to St. Matthew)
Italy/France

1966 Titanus/Arco/Lux

CREDITS

Director: Pier Paolo Pasolini; *Producer:* Alfredo Bini; *Screenplay:* Pier Paolo Pasolini; *Photography:* Tonino Delli Colli; *Music:* Luis Enrique Bacalov (*using compositions by* Johann Sebastian Bach, Wolfgang Amadeus Mozart, Sergei Prokofiev, Anton Webern); *Film Editor:* Nino Baragli; *Art Director:* Luigi Scaccianoce; *Costumes:* Danilo Donati; *Special Effects:* Ettore Catallucci; *Makeup:* Marcello Ceccarelli. *Running Time:* 136 minutes.

CAST

Enrique Irazoqui played *Jesus* in a cast that included: Margherita Caruso (*Mary, as a Girl*); Susanna Pasolini (*Mary, as a Woman*); Marcello Morante (*Joseph*); Mario Socrate (*John the Baptist*); Settimo Di Porto (*Peter*); Otello Sestill (*Judas*); Ferruccio Nuzzo (*Matthew*); Giacomo Morante (*John*); Alfonso Gatto (*Andrew*); Enzo Siciliano (*Simon*); Giorgio Agamben (*Philip*); Guido Cerretani (*Bartholomew*); Luigi Barbini (*James, Son of Alpheus*); Marcello Galdini (*James, Son of Zebedee*); Elio Spaziani (*Thaddeus*); Rosario Migale (*Thomas*); Rodolfo Wilcock (*Caiaphas*); Alessandro Tasca (*Pontius Pilate*); Amerigo Bevilacqua (*Herod the Great*); Francesco Leonetti (*Herod Antipas*); Franca Cupane (*Herodius*); Paola Tedesco (*Salomé*); Rossana Di Rocco (*Angel*); Eliseo Boschi (*Joseph of Arimathea*); Natalia Ginzburg (*Mary of Bethany*); Renato Terra (*A Pharisee*); Enrico Maria Salerno (*Voice of Jesus*).

COMMENTARY

Controversial filmmaker Pier Paolo Pasolini

THE GREATEST STORY EVER TOLD: The Resurrection. Pat Boone is at right.

THE GOSPEL ACCORDING TO ST. MATTHEW: Enrique Irazoqui (center) as Jesus at the Last Supper.

wrote and directed this surprisingly earnest 1964 Italian film adaptation of Jesus's life, *The Gospel According to St. Matthew*, which was released two years later in America to enthusiastic critical response. Pasolini had dealt with the subject of Christ before, allegorically, in the Italian anthology *RoGoPag* (1963), which contained a satiric episode in which the loutish conduct of a movie crew (led by Orson Welles, playing the director), shooting a version of the Passion Play, is contrasted with the serious material they are filming.

In *The Gospel According to St. Matthew*, Pasolini's own approach to the subject is sincere, unconventional, and almost entirely successful. Adapting his screenplay wholly from the Gospel of Matthew (thereby achieving a consistency of viewpoint lacking in most such films), and working with a cast of nonprofessionals featuring Enrique Irazoqui as Jesus, Pasolini manages to create, on a limited budget and in black-and-white, a completely believable milieu.

Whereas most Hollywood religious epics spend millions on accurate props, costumes, and huge sets, Pasolini achieves a pictorial verisimilitude that many of the more expensive biblical films lack, simply by shooting on a few well-chosen locations and dressing his performers in garb that, while historically indeterminate, *appears* to be correct. The quite genuine

164

THE GOSPEL ACCORDING TO ST. MATTHEW: Enrique Irazoqui (right).

THE GOSPEL ACCORDING TO ST. MATTHEW

THE GOSPEL ACCORDING TO ST. MATTHEW

spiritual feeling of the picture is intensified as a result, most apparent when Jesus miraculously cures a leper. The resulting transformation is shown by a simple, direct cut accompanied by a sudden burst of music. This technically crude effect is totally believable and accepted without question by the viewer. The music score for *The Gospel According to St. Matthew*, arranged by Luis Enrique Bacalov, is also excellent, incorporating classical music and spiritual hymns, with Tonino Delli Colli's stark black-and-white photography enhancing the atmosphere.

165

Pier Paolo Pasolini has made a pic poles apart from the many which have told the story of Christ. . . . The unconventional approach is rapidly accepted, and the pic acquires the look of a pageant—such as those enacted by citizens of many European villages every year—lensed in depth. Several times, the film soars to heights—as in the Calvary sequence, a masterful achievement which has the graphic immediacy of a newsreel document in a crescendo of tragedy and sorrow which is eminently moving and believable.

Variety

The viewer . . . has the mystical sense of being there.

New York Times

THE GOSPEL ACCORDING TO ST. MATTHEW: The betraying kiss of Judas; Otello **Sestill** (left) and Enrique Irazoqui.

THE GOSPEL ACCORDING TO ST. MATTHEW

166

SEDUTO ALLA SUR DESTRA
(Black Jesus)

Italian

1968 Ital Noleggio Cinematografica–
Castoro Films

CREDITS

Director: Valerio Zurlini; *Producer:* Carlo Lizzani; *Executive Producer:* N. E. Krisman; *Photography (Technicolor and Techniscope):* Aiace Parolin; *Screenplay:* Valerio Zurlini, Franco Brusati (*from a story by* Zurlini); *Music:* Ivan Vandor; *Film Editor:* Franco Aralli; *Art Direction and Costumes:* Franco Bottari; *Sound:* Pietro Spadoni. *Running Time:* 100 minutes.

CAST

Woody Strode (*Maurice Lalubi*); Franco Citti (*Oreste*); Jean Servais (*Mercenary Commander*); Pier Paolo Capponi (*Sergeant*); Stephen Forsyth (*Violent Prisoner*); WITH Luciano Lorcas, Salvo Basile, Silvio Fiore, Giuseppe Transocchi, Mirella Panfili, Renzo Rossi.

COMMENTARY

This obscure allegory, directed and cowritten by Valerio Zurlini, was intended to be a fictionalized documentation of the last days of African revolutionary Patrice Lumumba as a forty-minute segment in a five-part film called *Rage in Love.* It ultimately was developed into a feature-length screenplay combining the political career of Lumumba with the Passion of Christ. It premiered at the 1968 Cannes Film Festival but found no interest outside of Italy, despite the participation of veteran black actor Woody Strode in an unusual (and very rare) starring role.

With the surprise box-office success in the early seventies of black-oriented movies, Zurlini's film subsequently was acquired by a small American film distributor, Plaza Pictures, dubbed into English, shortened slightly to play down the Lumumba aspects, and given an American title, *Black Jesus,* along with an advertising campaign geared to black moviegoers. Strode's role as an imprisoned visionary African leader is clearly intended to represent Jesus Christ, and another character, Franco Citti's

Oreste, a half-mad thief also held captive in the prison, is apparently a Barabbas surrogate.

REVIEWS

Where original limitations might have helped carry off [Zurlini's] vision of a Black Christ, betrayed by a Black Judas to save colonial Philistines, the added length serves to highlight deficiencies and dissipates synthetic quality. . . . Zurlini, known for his poetic images, directs with an elementary touch that negates his high purpose. Religious symbolism is heavy-handed and uninspired, even elementary in most instances. Violence is excessive to the point of Grand Guignol.

Variety

It is not unlikely that Woody Stroke, a stalwart and capable actor . . . will now achieve star ranking. Certainly his characterization of a black leader with a charismatic hold over a host of followers has an unexpected gentleness, and he gives the Christ-like sufferings he is subjected to a strange dignity. . . . For those not too squeamish to find New Testament parallels, it's all pretty much there: the colonel as Pontius Pilate (played well by Jean Servais), Franco Citti as the good thief. There is a black Judas, and a black soldier cooperating with the white (and black) authorities serves as the actual killer, but it is done by knife and not crucifixion. The film makes no attempt to propagandize one way or the other; rather, it presents a bloody equation of our time with an event (perhaps myth) of two thousand years ago.

Saturday Review
September 11, 1971

What can a 12-year-old learn from *Black Jesus?* If he is black, he can learn that his people have a beautiful nobility . . . that comes from being oppressed and that his people can only maintain this nobility if they remain forever passive. If white, he can learn that he belongs to a race of hopelessly aggressive people; that he is guilty of an insurmountable number of crimes against blacks, and that, because of this, the nobility is forever denied him. . . . These are dangerous lessons. The one-dimensional treatment of man's most complex problems cheapens both black and whites.

Chicago Sun-Times

LA VOIE LACTEE
(The Milky Way)

France

1969 Greenwich-Fraia /U-M

CREDITS

Director: Luis Buñuel; *Producer:* Serge Silberman;

BLACK JESUS: Woody Strode.

Screenplay: Luis Buñuel, Jean Claude Carriere; *Photography* (*Eastmancolor*): Christian Matras; *Music:* Luis Buñuel; *Film Editor:* Louisette Hautecoeur; *Art Director:* Pierre Guffroy; *Costumes:* Jacqueline Guyot, Francoise Toumafond; *Makeup:* Jacqueline Pipard. *Running Time:* 105 minutes.

CAST

Bernard Verley played *Jesus* in a cast that included: Paul Frankeur (*Pierre*); Laurent Terzieff (*Jean*); Alain Cuny (*Man with Cape*); Edith Scob (*Virgin Mary*); Francois Maistre (*French Priest*); Claude Cerval (*Brigadier*); Muni (*Mother Superior*); Julien Bertheau (*Maitre d'Hotel*); Ellen Bahl (*Mme. Garnier*); Michel Piccoli (*The Marquis*); Agnes Capri (*Lamartine Institution Directress*); Michel Etcheverry (*The Inquisitor*); Pierre Clementi (*The Devil/Angel of Death*); Georges Marchal (*The Jesuit*); Jean Piat (*The Jansenist*); Denis Manuel (*Rodolphe*); Daniel Pilon (*Francois*); Claudio Brook (*Bishop*); Julien Guiomar (*Spanish Priest*); Marcel Peres (*Spanish Innkeeper*); Delphine Seyrig (*Prostitute*); Jean-Claude Carriere (*Priscillian*); Christine Simon (*Therese*); Augusta Carriere (*Sister Francoise*); Jean-David Ehrmann (*Condemned Man*); Pierre Lary (*Young Monk*); Bernard Musson (*French Innkeeper*); Michel Dacquin (*Mons. Garnier*); Gabriel Gobin (*Father*); Pierre Maguelon (*Civil Guard Corporal*); Marius Laurey (*Blind Man*); Jean Clarieux (*Apostle Peter*); Christian Van Cau (*Apostle Andrew*); Claudine Berg (*Mother*); Rita Maiden, Beatrice Constantini (*Priscillian's Daughters*); Claude Jetter (*Virgin in Spanish Inn*); Jacqueline Rouillard (*Restaurant Maid*); José Bergosa (*Priscillian's First Deacon*); Douking (*Shepherd*); WITH Jean-Louis Broust, Stephane Bouy, Michel Creton, Raoul Delfosse, Jean Dhermay, Pascal Fardoulis, Paul Pavel, Douglas Read, Jacques Rispal, Cesar Torres.

COMMENTARY

Unconventional director Luis Buñuel's allegorical fantasy *The Milky Way*, featuring Bernard Verley as Jesus, is an irreverent parable that forsakes linear narrative in favor of probing characterization and symbolic intellectual concepts. The picture follows two men as they journey to a religious shrine in Spain, with most of the supporting characters they encounter on their trip representing (in Buñuel's opinion) the diverse heresies, both cultural and spiritual, in modern civilization. Buñuel long had dealt with potentially controversial (some would say blasphemous) religious attitudes in his films, going back as far as *Un Chien Andalou* in 1928, but since his works usually have been screened in "art houses" and seldom have received wide distribution, they have never provoked the massive criticism aimed at mainstream productions like *The Last Temptation of Christ* of two decades hence.

REVIEWS

An immense, unusual, witty, comic and brilliant probing of religion in general and Catholic aspects in particular.

Variety

"Thank God, I am still an atheist," claims director Luis Buñuel. On that rock he has built his crutch—a lifelong obsession with Spanish Catholicism.... With *The Milky Way*, the grand old unbeliever returns to his favorite theme in a magical mystery tour of the dogma, hypocrisy and glories of Christianity.... Cluttered with Buñuel's standard paraphernalia of stigmata, deformity, mud and fire, *The Milky Way* offers no unified vision, no system of thought or style.

Time

Buñuel employs no fantastic effects, though this is a livelier fantasy than, say, *The Wizard of Oz*.

New York Times

MORE FILMS OF THE 1960s

Herod the Great (Allied Artists, 1960) was a dubbed Italian spectacle covering the last years of the insane tyrant and his death after the birth of Jesus Christ. Starring Edmund Purdom, the film—produced as *Le Roi Cruel* (*The Cruel King*)—was made in 1958 but did not find an American distributor for two years. In its December 14, 1960, review, *Variety* commented: "Slowly, but surely, the Italian film industry appears to be piecing together a sort of history of the ancient world on twentieth-century celluloid, draining the last ounce of melodrama out of the sacred scriptures and historical records of the period just B. C. In director Arnaldo Genoino's *Herod the Great*, a grim, ponderous account of the ravings and cravings of that mad monarch, a key piece in this quasi-biblical, quasi-historical jigsaw is fit into place for the modern filmgoer who seeks periodic escape in these oversexed, overstuffed costume epics."

In *Mary Magdalene* (Amex, 1960), another dubbed Italian effort, American star Yvonne De Carlo (who had been featured in DeMille's 1956 *The Ten Commandments*) portrayed the title courtesan. The screenplay (by director Carlo Ludovico Bragadia) was not derived from biblical events at all, and was a completely fictionalized melodrama, with Mary renouncing her wanton past after seeing a vision of Jesus. Instead of exploiting the rich material in the Bible, the picture settles for using familiar biblical names as mere window dressing; Mary's brother, for instance, is named Lazarus. This wide-screen color film was produced in 1958 as *La Spade e La Croce* (*The Sword and the Cross*).

The Redeemer (Empire Pictures, 1965) was a Spanish production filmed in 1959 under the title *Los Mysterios Del Rosario* (*The Mysteries of the Rosary*). Produced by Rev. Patrick Payton, it was shot near Madrid and examined the last three days in the life of Christ (Luis Alvarez). Jesus's face is never shown on-screen, and the familiar voice of Hollywood veteran Macdonald Carey overdubbed Jesus's dialogue in the reedited American version, which was narrated by Sebastian Cabot.

THE MILKY WAY: Bernard Verley (right) as Jesus, with Claudio Brook.

170

CHAPTER 7

THE NINETEEN SEVENTIES

JOHNNY GOT HIS GUN

1971 Cinemation

CREDITS

Director: Dalton Trumbo; *Producer:* Bruce Campbell; *Screenplay:* Dalton Trumbo (*based on his novel*); *Photography* (*Eastmancolor*): Jules Brenner; *Music:* Jerry Fielding; *Film Editor:* William P. Dornish; *Production Design:* Harold Michelson; *Costumes:* Theodora Van Runkle; *Associate Producers:* Tony Monaco, Christopher Trumbo. *Running Time:* 111 minutes.

CAST

Timothy Bottoms (*Joe Bonham*); Kathy Fields (*Karen*); Marsha Hunt (*Joe's Mother*); Jason Robards (*Joe's Father*); Donald Sutherland ("*Christ*"); Diane Varsi (*Fourth Nurse*); Sandy Brown Wyeth (*Lucky*); Donald Barry (*Jody Simmons*); Peter Brocco (*Ancient Prelate*); Kendell Clarke (*Hospital Official*); Eric Christmas (*Corporal Timlon*); Eduard Franz (*Colonel/General Tillery*); Craig Bovia (*Little Guy*); Judy Howard Chaikin (*Bakery Girl*); Robert Cole (*Orator*); Maurice Dallimore (*British Colonel*); Robert Easton (*Third Doctor*); Larry Fleischman (*Russ*); Tony Geary (*Redhead*); Edmund Gilbert (*Priest*); Ben Hammer (*Second Doctor*); Milton Barnes (*First Reader*); Wayne Heffley (*Captain*); Lynn Hanratty (*Elizabeth at six*); Ernestine Johnston (*Farm Woman*); Joseph Kaufman (*Rudy*); Mike Lee (*Bill*); Kerry MacLane (*Joe at ten*)); Charles McGraw (*Mike*); William Mims (*Gentleman*); Byron Morrow (*Brigadier General*); Alice Nunn, Marge Redmond, Jodean Russo (*Nurses*); David Soul (*Swede*); Etienne Veazie (*Black Boy*); Peter Virgo, Jr. (*Attendant*); Gigy Vorgan (*Catherine at thirteen*); Jeff Walker (*Fifth Guy*); Bruce Watson (*Technician*); Cynthia Wilson (*Catherine at seven*); Sandy Brownwyeth (*Lucky*).

COMMENTARY

In *Johnny Got His Gun*, Donald Sutherland appeared as a Christ figure in a dream sequence occurring in the mind of a horribly mutilated, bedridden war veteran. A quadruple amputee totally incapacitated by his injuries, the maimed soldier (Timothy Bottoms) can escape reality only by immersion in his own fantasies, and at one point he imagines himself conversing with Jesus. Directed and

JOHNNY GOT HIS GUN:
Donald Sutherland.

JOHNNY GOT HIS GUN: Kathy Fields and Timothy Bottoms.

written by Dalton Trumbo, who based the screenplay on his own 1938 novel, *Johnny Got His Gun* is a disturbing antiwar diatribe produced at the height of public opposition to the Vietnam conflict. Although apparently sincere, like many films of that period it has not dated well. Originally, director Luis Buñuel

JOHNNY GOT HIS GUN: Donald Sutherland.

172

had planned to direct a film based on the book in 1965, and when that production failed to materialize, another version was nearly made by Warner Bros. Trumbo eventually filmed it on his own with funds from private sources, shooting the picture in forty-two days on a budget of only $750,000. It originally ran more than three hours, but was edited down to less than two before release.

Trumbo claimed that the portion of the story dealing with the Timothy Bottoms character's boyhood was autobiographical, and stated that he first conceived the basic premise of the novel in 1933, when he read of a recently deceased World War I British officer who had been so badly disfigured that the authorities kept his survival a secret for fifteen years, telling his family that he had died in combat.

REVIEWS

Dalton Trumbo has distilled, both as scripter and director, a touching, moving film.

Variety

A mess of cliched, imprecise sentimentalizing and fantasizing . . . the work of a Norman Rockwell who couldn't draw.

New York Times

[Trumbo's] passionate antiwar sermon has arrived at a time when the sermon has been done often and better and, more to the point, has long since been accepted by the congregation.

Los Angeles Times

THE RULING CLASS

Great Britain
1972 Avco Embassy

CREDITS

Producers: Jules Buck, Jack Hawkins; *Director:* Peter Medak; *Screenplay:* Peter Barnes (*based on his play*); *Photography (DeLuxe Color):* Ken Hodges; *Music:*

THE RULING CLASS: Peter O'Toole (center).

John Cameron; *Film Editor:* Ray Lovejoy; *Production Design:* Peter Murton; *Costumes:* Ruth Myers; *Special Effects:* Roy Whybrow; *Choreography:* Eleanor Fazan; *Makeup:* Charles Parker. *Running Time:* 154 minutes. (Originally shown in the U.S. at 130 minutes.)

CAST

Peter O'Toole (*Jack, 14th Earl of Gurney*); Alastair Sim (*Bishop Lampton*); Arthur Lowe (*Tucker*); Harry Andrews (*13th Earl of Gurney*); Coral Browne (*Lady Claire Gurney*); Michael Bryant (*Dr. Herder*); Nigel Green (*McKyle*); William Mervyn (*Sir Charles Gurney*); Carolyn Seymour (*Grace Shelly*); James Villiers (*Dinsdale Gurney*); Hugh Burden (*Matthew Peake*); Graham Crowden (*Truscott*); Kay Walsh (*Mrs. Piggot-Jones*); Patsy Byrne (*Mrs. Treadwell*); Joan Cooper (*Nurse Brice*); James Grout (*Inspector*); Margaret Lacey (*Midwife*); James Hazeldine (*Detective Sgt. Fraser*); Hugh Owens (*Toastmaster*); Griffith Davies, Oliver MacGreevy, Henry Woolf (*Inmates*); Neil Kennedy (*Dr. Herder's Assistant*); Julian D'Albie, Llewellyn Rees, Ronald Adam, Kenneth Benda (*Lords*); WITH Declan Mulholland, Cyril Appleton, Leslie Schofield.

174

COMMENTARY

Peter O'Toole starred as an insane heir to a fortune who believes that he is Jesus Christ. No facet of British society escapes the corrosive scrutiny of this biting satire, undeniably funny in its merciless indictment of upper-class pretense and hypocrisy. Directed by Peter Medak and scripted by Peter Barnes from his own play, the film, although too long and a bit excessive at times, does manage to avoid the tiresome conceits that often hamper satires of this type, and the cast was excellent, with O'Toole nominated for an Oscar as Best Actor. Particularly effective is the darkly humorous concluding punchline, in which, the O'Toole character seemingly "cured" of his messianic delusions, he announces that his name is "Jack"—after which it's revealed that he now believes himself to be Jack the Ripper!

REVIEWS

A splendid cast, top physical and technical

THE RULING CLASS: Peter O'Toole, with Patsy Byrne (left) and Joan Cooper.

trimmings, spell achievement for its makers in bringing off a slice of qualitative entertainment.

Variety

Mr. Barnes has written *The Ruling Class*, and Mr. Medak has directed it, in a whiz-bang, vaudeville ("get 'em on and off quickly") style, employing songs, dances and gags that sometimes shock but never completely disguise the fundamental ordinariness of the ideas.

New York Times

THE GOSPEL ROAD

1973 20th Century-Fox

CREDITS

Director: Robert Elfstrom; *Producers:* Johnny Cash, June Carter Cash; *Screenplay:* Johnny Cash, Larry

THE RULING CLASS: Carolyn Seymour and Peter O'Toole.

175

THE GOSPEL ROAD: Robert Elfstrom.

Murray; *Photography* (*Eastmancolor*): Robert Elfstrom, Tom McDonough; *Music:* Larry Butler; *Film Editor:* John Craddock; *Lyrics:* John Denver, Larry Gatlin, Kris Kristofferson, Joe South, Harold and Don Reid, Christopher Wren, Johnny Cash. *Running Time:* 93 minutes.

CAST

Robert Elfstrom played *Jesus* in a cast that included: June Carter Cash (*Mary Magdalene*); Larry Lee (*John the Baptist*); Paul Smith (*Peter*); Alan Dater (*Nicodemus*); Robert Elfstrom, Jr. (*Christ Child*); Gelles La-Blanc (*John*); Terrance Winston Mannock (*Matthew*); Thomas Leventhal (*Judas*); John Paul Kay (*James the Elder*); Sean Armstrong (*Thomas*); Lyle Nicholson (*Andrew*); Steven Chernoff (*Philip*); Stuart Clark (*Nathaniel*); Ulf Pollack (*Thaddeus*); Jonathan Sanders (*Simon*).

COMMENTARY

The Gospel Road was a pseudo-documentary look at Jesus's life produced by country singer Johnny Cash, who also narrated. Robert Elfstrom played Jesus and directed the picture, which, although well-intentioned, fell prey to occasional miscalculation: during the Crucifixion, modern views of the polluted environment are intercut with the action. While the visual counterpoint served as effective social commentary in this instance, the technique was weakened by constant repetition throughout the film.

The Gospel Road was enhanced by location footage of Cash shot in Jerusalem, with the singer pointing out historic landmarks to the viewer.

176

The Gospel Road is an admirable musical documentary filmed in Israel, about the public life of Jesus Christ.

Variety

The basic problem with the production is that the director tends to work an interesting idea to death. But with all its limitations, *The Gospel Road* presents the real Jesus as he might have been.

Christianity Today

GODSPELL

1973 Columbia

CREDITS

Director: David Greene; *Producer:* Edgar Lansbury; *Screenplay:* David Greene, John-Michael Tebelak (*based on the musical play by* Tebelek *and* Stephen Schwartz); *Photography (TVC color):* Richard G. Heimann; *Music:* Stephen Schwartz; *Lyrics:* Stephen Schwartz, Jay Hamburger, Peggy Gordon; *Film Editor:* Alan Heim; *Production Designer:* Brian Eatwell; *Art Director:* Ben Kasazkow; *Costumes:* Sherrie Sucher; *Choreography:* Sam Bayes. *Running Time:* 103 minutes.

CAST

Victor Garber played *Jesus* in a cast that included: David Haskell (*John/Judas*); Jerry Sroka (*Jerry*); Lynne Thigpen (*Lynne*); Katie Hanley (*Katie*); Robin Lamont (*Robin*); Gilmer McCormick (*Gilmer*); Joanne Jonas (*Joanne*); Merrell Jackson (*Merrell*); Jeffrey Mylett (*Jeffrey*).

COMMENTARY

An overly simplistic, highly stylized musical adaptation of the Gospel of St. Matthew, *Godspell* was based on a dramatic stage play by John-Michael Tebelek, with songs added later by Stephen Schwartz. An impressionistic view of Jesus, shot in New York City amidst contemporary urban backgrounds, with Victor Garber playing Christ in clown makeup and a Superman T-shirt, the film typifies much of what was wrong with popular entertainment at that time, with the complexities of the Bible reduced to puerile social commentary (Jesus "crucified" on a cyclone fence) and facile mugging from the performers. Seen today, *Godspell* is very much a relic of a bygone time, and although fascinating on that unintended level, the film is redeemed only by a couple of lively songs and the occasionally inventive photography.

There is nothing wrong with a modern, free-form adaptation of the Gospels; interpreting Jesus's story in contemporary terms is not a new concept. (Artists of the Middle Ages frequently painted biblical scenes with the figures garbed in then-contemporary fashion.) The most important element is sincerity, and that is, unfortunately, what is most lacking in *Godspell*.

REVIEWS

A relentlessly simplistic approach to the New Testament interpreted in overbearing children's-theatre-style mugging . . . . Overall acting style comes across as cloying excess.

Variety

It's not about religion or philosophy but show business, and its frame—the life and death of Jesus reenacted in contemporary Manhattan and environs—is hardly more than a gimmick to allow the show's authors to help themselves to some lovely original material never protected by copyright.

New York Times

JESUS CHRIST, SUPERSTAR

1973 Universal

CREDITS:

Director: Norman Jewison; *Producers:* Norman Jewison, Robert Stigwood; *Screenplay:* Norman Jewison, Melvyn Bragg (*based on the musical play with book and lyrics by* Tim Rice *and music by* Andrew Lloyd Webber); *Photography (Technicolor):* Douglas Slocombe; *Music Director:* André Previn; *Film Editor:* Anthony

GODSPELL: Victor Garber (left) as Jesus, with David Haskell as Judas.

GODSPELL: Victor Garber.

GODSPELL: Victor Garber (left of center).

GODSPELL: A musical number with Victor Garber (center).

JESUS CHRIST, SUPERSTAR: Ted Neely (center) and the Apostles.

Gibbs; *Production Designer:* Richard MacDonald; *Choreography:* Rob Iscove; *Costumes:* Yvonne Blake. *Running Time:* 107 minutes.

CAST

Ted Neely played *Jesus* in a cast that included: Carl Anderson (*Judas Iscariot*); Yvonne Elliman (*Mary Magdalene*); Barry Dennen (*Pontius Pilate*); Bob Bingham (*Caiaphas*); Larry T. Marshall (*Simon Zealotes*); Joshua Mostel (*King Herod*); Kurt Yahgiian (*Annas*); Phillip Toubus (*Peter*); Pi Douglas, Jonathan Wynne, Richard Molinare, Jeffrey Hyslop, Robert LuPone, Thommie Walsh, David Devit, Richard Orbach, Shoold Wagner (*Apostles*); Darcel Wynne, Sally Neal, Vera Biloshisky, Wendy Maltby, Baay-

JESUS CHRIST, SUPERSTAR: Ted Neely as Jesus, with Yvonne Elliman as Mary Magdalene.

ork Lee, Susan Allanson, Ellen Hoffman, Judith Daby, Adayoa Pio, Marcia McBroom, Leeyan Granger, Kathryn Wright, Denise Pence, Wyetta Turner, Tamar Zafria, Rild Oren, Lea Kestin (*Women*); Zvulun Cohen, Meir Israel, Itzhak Sidranski, David Rfjwan, Amity Razi, Avi Ben-Haim, Haim Bashi, David Duack (*Priests*); Steven Bockvor, Peter Luria, David Barkan, Danny Basevitch, Cliff Michaelevski, Tom Guest, Stephen Denenberg, Didi Liekov (*Roman Soldiers*); Doron Gaash, Naom Cohen, Zvi Lehat, Moshe Uziel (*Temple Guards*).

COMMENTARY

Offering beautiful location filming in Israel, *Jesus Christ, Superstar* was the most financially successful entry in the bizarre and short-lived subgenre of musical religious pictures. Directed by Norman Jewison from the popular rock opera with a score by Tim Rice and Andrew Lloyd Webber, the film stars Ted Neely as Jesus, with Yvonne Elliman as Mary Magdalene and Carl Anderson as Judas. Both Elliman and Anderson are good (there was a degree of controversy generated at the time over the casting of a black man as Judas), but Neely is curiously weak as Jesus, and now that the film's cultural moment has passed, he looks faintly ridiculous bursting spontaneously into falsetto song. Most of the music is pleasant, though, and seems more effective than the film itself, leading one to the conclusion that *Jesus Christ, Superstar* has more significance as a record album than as a motion picture.

The film was hugely successful, grossing nearly $20 million. It earned its only Oscar nomination for André Previn's musical direction. Andrew Lloyd Webber later, of course, went on to write the successful musicals *Cats*, *Evita*, *The Phantom of the Opera*, and *Aspects of Love*, among others.

REVIEWS

. . . Veers from elegantly simple through forced metaphor to outright synthetic in dramatic impact.

Variety

JESUS CHRIST, SUPERSTAR: The Last Supper.

Broadway and Israel meet head on and disastrously in the movie version of the rock opera.

New York Times

Jesus Christ, Superstar, though a theological disaster, has become an economical triumph. . . . What we need, however, is a Christian filmmaker to produce the true story.

Christianity Today

Zalman King played *Jesus* (*Yeshua*) in a cast that included: Harry Andrews (*Yohanan the Baptist*); Hugh Griffith (*Caiaphas*); Donald Pleasence (*Pontius Pilate*); Scott Wilson (*Judas*); Dan Ades (*Andros*); Michael Baseleon (*Mattai*); Lewis van Bergen (*Yoram*); William Burns (*Shiman*); Daniel Hedaya (*Yaacov*); Helena Kallianiotes (*A Visionary Woman*); Kevin O'Connor (*Irijah*); Robert Walker (*Bar Talmi*); William Watson (*Roman Captain*).

COMMENTARY

The Passover Plot offered a revisionist view of Jesus (here referred to under the Hebraic name

JESUS CHRIST, SUPERSTAR: Ted Neely.

THE PASSOVER PLOT

1976 Atlas Films

CREDITS

Director: Michael Campus; *Producer:* Wolf Schmidt; *Executive Producer:* Menahem Golan; *Associate Producer:* Yoram Globus; *Screenplay:* Millard Cohan, Patricia Knop (*based on the book by* Dr. Hugh J. Schonfield); *Photography* (*DeLuxe Color*): Adam Greenberg; *Music:* Alex North; *Film Editor:* Dov Hoenig; *Art Director:* Kuli Sander; *Costumes:* Mary Wills; *Special Effects:* Jack Rabin; *Sound:* Cyril Collick. *Running Time:* 108 minutes.

JESUS CHRIST, SUPERSTAR: King Herod (Joshua Mostel, center) and his court.

"Yeshua") as a political radical who plans his own crucifixion in a plot against the Romans. Derived from the controversial book of the same title by Hugh J. Schonfield, the film postulates that Jesus intended to survive the Crucifixion through the use of anesthetic drugs, faking his own Resurrection as a ploy to inspire his followers in a revolt against the Romans, and that he died on the cross unintentionally when impaled by a Roman soldier's spear, and never actually arose from the dead. Schonfield's book, although well-researched in terms of historical detail, indulged in wild theorizing and was blatantly dogmatic in approach. The movie itself failed to ignite mass criticism only because it was such an abject failure at the box office. Michael Campus's direction was sluggish, and Zalman King made a transparent, ineffectual Jesus.

REVIEWS

. . . Drains the vitality out of the Christ story through excessive verbiage and monotonous overacting.

Variety

A silly movie made from that bad book by Hugh Schonfield so much talked about a few years ago. . . . Most of the actors are television rejects.

Christianity Today

JESUS OF NAZARETH

*1977 Sir Lew Grade Productions/
ITC/RAI-Television for NBC*

CREDITS

Director: Franco Zeffirelli; *Producer:* Vincenzo Labella; *Executive Producer:* Bernard J. Kingham; *Associate Producer:* Dyson Lovell; *Screenplay:* Anthony Burgess, Suso Cecchi d'Amico, Franco Zeffirelli; *Photography (color):* Armando Nennuzzi, David Watkins; *Music:* Maurice Jarre; *Art Director:* Gianni Quaranta; *Scenic Design:* Francesco Fedeli; *Film Editor:* Reginald Mills; *Choreography:* Alberto Testa; *Costumes:* Marcel Escoffier, Enrico Sabbatini; *Additional Dialogue:* David Butler. *Running Time:* 397 minutes. *Premiere Dates:* April 3, 10, 1977. (Originally shown in six and one-half hours on two nights; later expanded to eight hours over four nights)

CAST

Robert Powell played *Jesus* in a cast that included: Anne Bancroft (*Mary Magdalene*); Ernest Borgnine (*The Centurion*); Claudia Cardinale (*The Adulteress*); Valentina Cortese (*Herodias*); James Farentino (*Simon Peter*); James Earl Jones (*Balthazar*); Stacy Keach (*Barabbas*); Tony Lo Bianco (*Quintilius*); James Mason (*Joseph of Arimathea*); Ian McShane (*Judas*); Laurence Olivier (*Nicodemus*); Donald Pleasence (*Melchior*); Christopher Plummer (*Herod Antipas*); Anthony Quinn (*Caiaphas*); Fernando Rey (*Gaspar*); Ralph Richardson (*Simeon*); Rod Steiger (*Pontius Pilate*); Peter Ustinov (*Herod the Great*); Michael York (*John the Baptist*); Olivia Hussey (*The Virgin Mary*);

JESUS CHRIST, SUPERSTAR: The suicide of Judas (Carl Anderson).

THE PASSOVER PLOT: **Zalman King** (foreground) as Jesus.

Cyril Cusack (*Rabbi Yehuda*); Ian Holm (*Zerah*); Yorgo Voyagis (*Joseph*); Ian Bannen (*Amos*); Regina Bianchi (*Anna*); Marina Berti (*Elizabeth*); Oliver Tobias (*Joel*); Maria Carta (*Martha*); Lee Montague (*Habbukuk*); Renato Rascel (*The Blind Man*); Norman Bowler (*Saturninus*); Robert Beatty (*Proculus*); John Phillips (*Naso*); Ken Jones (*Jotham*); Nancy Nevinson (*Abigail*); Renato Terra (*Abel*); Roy Holder (*Enoch*); Jonathan Adams (*Adam*); Christopher Reich (*Circumcision Priest*); Lorenzo Monet (*Jesus at twelve*); Robert Davey (*Daniel*); Oliver Smith (*Saul*); George Camiller (*Hosias*); Murray Salem (*Simon the Zealot*); Tony Vogel (*Andrew*); Isabel Mestres (*Salomé*); Michael Cronin (*Eliphaz*); Forbes Collins (*Jonas*); Steve Gardner (*Philip*); John Duttine (*John the Evangelist*); Michael Haughey (*Nahum*); Keith Skinner (*Obsessed Boy*); Cyril Shaps (*Obsessed Boy's Father*); Jonathan Müller (*James*); John Tordoff (*Malachi*);

JESUS OF NAZARETH (1977): From left: Frank De Wolfe, Anne Bancroft, James Mason, and Robert Powell.

186

JESUS OF NAZARETH (1977): Robert Powell.

Keith Washington (*Matthew*); Sergio Nicolai (*James II*); Antonello Campodifiori (*Ircanus*); Renato Montalbano (*Jairus*); Bruce Liddington (*Thomas*); Mimmo Crao (*Thaddeus*); Derek Godfrey (*Elihu*).

COMMENTARY

Director Franco Zeffirelli's reverent, star-packed *Jesus of Nazareth* was telecast on NBC in two segments, and the six-hour and thirty-seven-minute film is, overall, the finest adaptation of Jesus's life ever made. Zeffirelli's production was initially embroiled in controversy after the director had made an unfortunate public statement about Christ's humanity being emphasized in the film; the movie was immediately attacked by fundamentalist groups and religious leaders (none of whom had seen the film). A skittish General Motors

withdrew sponsorship of the program, but when *Jesus of Nazareth* was finally broadcast (with a new sponsor), the negative reaction against the film proved groundless. Not only was Jesus indeed shown as undeniably divine, but the picture was directed with such restraint, beauty, and obvious sincerity that it stood as something of a revelation in comparison to the many previous movie versions of the

JESUS OF NAZARETH (1977): Robert Powell.

JESUS OF NAZARETH (1977): Robert Powell.

JESUS OF NAZARETH (1977):
Robert Powell.

188

Savior's life. Best typifying Zeffirelli's thoughtful approach is his presentation of the Immaculate Conception, with the Virgin Mary (Olivia Hussey) bathed in a divine ray of moonlight. Plainly shot in almost total silence, the episode attains an intense spiritual quality too often absent from other films of this type. The screenplay, by novelist Anthony Burgess, Zeffirelli, and the latter's frequent collaborator, Suso Cecchi D'Amico, adheres most closely to the Gospel of John, and stresses Jesus's divinity as well as his humanity. While the Miracle at Cana and Jesus walking on water are omitted, we are shown the raising of Lazarus, the multiplying of fish and bread, the healing of a blind man, and the Resurrection. As Christ, not-overly-exposed British actor Robert Powell brings a powerful sensitivity to the role, successfully delineating the varied facets of Jesus's personality. Powell's Jesus is surprisingly forceful when he angrily denounces the religious hypocrites of the time. If there is one flaw in Zeffirelli's production, it is his unfortunate decision to use "name" actors in the supporting roles—Sir Laurence Olivier, Anthony Quinn, Rod Steiger, Anne Bancroft, James Mason, and Ernest Borgnine. Even so, this does no great harm to the film, and the fact that this profusion of "guest stars" never becomes the liability that it was in *The Greatest Story Ever Told* is only further testimony to Zeffirelli's directorial skill.

REVIEWS

Rarely have both the humanity and the divinity of Christ been evoked with as much passion, sensitivity and ecumenical deference as Zeffirelli has brought to the story.

Newsweek

Though slow-paced and a bit *too* reverent, the biopic was visually and dramatically interesting. Without doing violence to the New Testament, writers Anthony Burgess, Suso Cecchi D'Amico and Franco Zeffirelli managed to generate and maintain dramatic tension. The $18,000,000 that Lew Grade—whose ITC coproduced with Italy's RAI—invested was apparent in costuming and locale, and especially in the cast. Robert Powell gained authority in the title role as he built the character, though playing a Deity is obviously an impossibility for a mere human. No humor, nor even any irony, can be allowed to intrude.

Variety

As with all of Zeffirelli's work, from the film *Romeo and Juliet* to his theater and opera stagings, this new production combines minute details with rich visual effects.

New York Times

Zeffirelli has presented the life of Christ with taste and sensitivity. The acting, direction and photography are of the highest professional standards.

The Christian Century

The ingredient that sets this Jesus film apart from the others is its naturalness, its simplicity. The Gospels tell Jesus' story in simple, straightforward prose, with no purple passages or trumpet-like words. And Zeffirelli translated that style onto film.

Christianity Today

THE NATIVITY

1978 D'Angelo/Bullock/Allen Productions for 20th Century-Fox TV and ABC

CREDITS

Director: Bernard L. Kowalski; *Producer:* William P. D'Angelo; *Executive Producers:* Ray Allen, Harvey Bullock; *Screenplay:* Millard Kaufman, Mort Fine; *Photography (color):* Gabor Pogany; *Music:* Lalo Schifrin; *Film Editors:* Robert Phillips, Jerry Dronsky; *Art Director:* Luciano Spadoni. *Running Time:* 100 minutes.

CAST

Madeline Stowe (*Mary*); John Shea (*Joseph*); Jane Wyatt (*Anna*); Paul Stewart (*Zacharias*); Leo McKern

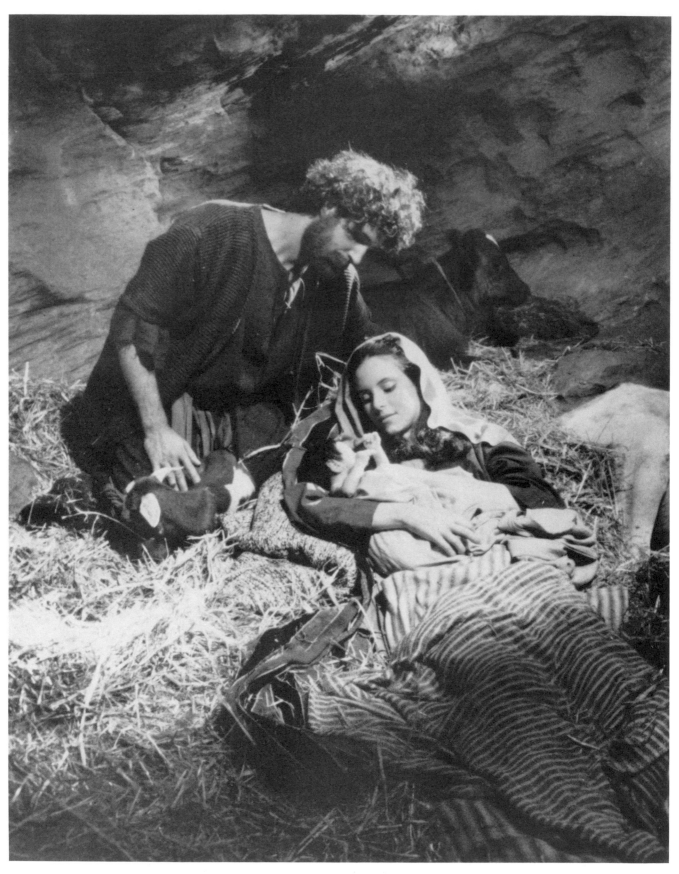

THE NATIVITY: John Shea and Madeline Stowe as Joseph and Mary with the newborn Jesus.

(*Herod*); Audrey Totter (*Elizabeth*); George Voskovec (*Joachim*); Julie Garfield (*Zipporah*); Kate O'Mara (*Salomé*); Barrie Houghton (*Preacher*); Jamil Zakkai (*Menachem*); Freddie Jones (*Diomedes*); John Rhys-Davies (*Nestor*); Morgan Shephard (*Flavius*); Geoffrey Beevers (*Eleazar*); Jacob Witkin (*Census Taker*); Jack Lynn (*Innkeeper*).

COMMENTARY

This unassuming made-for-tv movie was well-produced on a modest budget, and actress Madeline Stowe was especially good as the Virgin Mary. The direction by Bernard Kowalski is competent, and the film is nicely photographed by Gabor Pogany. Especially impressive is the movie's geographic authenticity and the sincere attempt by the producers to include appropriate ethnic types in the cast, which lends badly needed verisimilitude to the proceedings. Veteran character actor Leo McKern contributes a nice supporting performance as mad King Herod, fearful of the Saviour's impending birth. McKern's over-the-top theatricality is appropriate to the role but contrasts jarringly with the underplaying of the other actors. The film's sets, although economical, are for the most part convincing enough, if not entirely accurate in period detail.

REVIEW

Millard Kaufman and Mort Fine have fashioned a fine screenplay in their *The Nativity*. . . . Skillfully integrated in the tale is the contemporary drama of the times, the young revolutionaries of Israel resisting the Romans and Herod the mad king. . . . Madeline Stowe contributes a rich portrayal as Mary, and John Shea is ideally cast as Joseph.

Variety

MARY AND JOSEPH:
A STORY OF FAITH

1979 Astral Films/Lorimar Television for NBC

CREDITS

Director: Eric Till; *Producer:* Gene Corman; *Executive Producers:* Lee Rich, Harold Greenberg; *Screenplay:*

Carmen Culver; *Photography (color):* Adam Greenberg; *Music:* Robert Farnon; *Film Editor:* J. Howard Terrill; *Art Director:* John Blezard; *Sound:* Cyril Collick. *Running Time:* 180 minutes.

CAST

Blanche Baker (*Mary*); Jeff East (*Joseph*); Colleen Dewhurst (*Elizabeth*); Murray Matheson (*Zacharias*); Lloyd Bochner (*Matthew*); Shay Duffin (*Bartholomew*); Paul Hecht (*Joachim*); Marilyn Lightstone (*Anna*); Stephen McHattie (*Judah*); Tuvia Tavi (*Demetrius*); WITH Yossi Yadin, Liron Nirgod, Joseph Bee, Yehudh Ephroni, Dina Doran, Yakar Semach, Gabi Amroni, Israel Biderman, Amos Makadi, Noam Kedem, Jacob Ben Sira.

COMMENTARY

Another retelling of the Nativity, this made-for-tv movie, produced in Canada by Lorimar, is similar in basic concept to *The Nativity* but is inferior to that film, despite a larger budget. Leads Blanche Baker and Jeff East were both miscast in their roles, and the film is far too long at three hours. Certainly noteworthy as the *lengthiest* film version of the Nativity yet, the picture could have benefitted from tighter editing. The two leads, although competent enough in their roles, were simply unacceptable in an ethnic sense, looking far too Middle-American to be believable. While other productions of this sort were by this time striving for more authentic casting, *Mary and Joseph: A Story of Faith* looked and played like a regression to one of the more bland 1950s spectacles.

REVIEWS

This three-hour extravaganza reduces the biblical characters to cute types usually found in television commercials. Mary (Blanche Baker) vacillates between being a Barbie Doll and Tennessee Williams' *Baby Doll* [which starred her mother].

New York Times

Account of early days of Joseph and Mary has been blown up into an awkward, unmoving adventure filmed against magnificent locales of Israel, but all the authenticity of the backgrounds, all the genuineness of the

MARY AND JOSEPH: Blanche Baker and Jeff East.

costumes . . . can't bring the story to life; writer Carmen Culver and director Eric Till have managed to turn one of mankind's greatest stories into tedium. . . . Telefilm veers from contemporary viewpoints to historical posing, from pop to pap, with no sense of vivacity.

Variety

MONTY PYTHON'S LIFE OF BRIAN

Great Britain

1979 Warner Bros.

CREDITS

Director: Terry Jones; *Producer:* John Goldstone; *Screenplay:* Graham Chapman, John Cleese, Terry Gilliam, Eric Idle, Terry Jones, Michael Palin; *Photography (Color):* Peter Biziou; *Music:* Geoffrey Burgon, Andre Jacquemin, David Howman, Eric Idle; *Film Editor:* Julian Doyle; *Art Director:* Roger Christian; *Costumes:* Hazel Pethig, Charles Knode; *Animation Director:* Terry Gilliam. *Running Time:* 93 minutes.

CAST

Ken Colley played *Jesus* in a cast that included: Terry Jones (*The Virgin Mandy/The Mother of Brian, a Ratbag/Colin/Simon the Holy Man/Saintly Passerby*); Graham Chapman (*First Wise Man/Brian Called Brian/Biggus Dickus*); Michael Palin (*Second Wise Man/Mr. Big Nose/Francis, a Revolutionary/Mrs. A Who Casts the Second Stone/Ex-Leper/Ben, an Ancient Prisoner/Pontius Pilate, Roman Governor/A Boring Prophet/Eddie/Nisus Wettus*); John Cleese (*Third Wise Man/Reg. Leader of the Judean Peoples' Front/Jewish*

Official at the Stoning/Centurion of the Yard/Deadly Dirk/Arthur); Gwen Taylor (*Mrs. Big Nose/Woman with Sick Donkey/Young Girl*); Eric Idle (*Mr. Cheeky/ Stan Called Loretta, a Confused Revolutionary/Harry the Haggler, Beard and Stone Salesman/Culprit Woman Who Casts the First Stone/Intensely Dull Youth/Otto, the Nazarene Jailer's Assistant/Mr. Frisbee III*); Terence Baylor (*Gregory/Revolutionaries and Masked Commandos/Dennis*); Carol Cleveland (*Mrs. Gregory/ Elsie*); Charles McKeown (*Man Further Forward/ Revolutionaries and Masked Commandos/Roman Soldier Stig/Giggling Guard/A False Prophet/Blind Man*); Terry Gilliam (*Another Person Further Forward/Revolutionaries and Masked Commandos/A Blood and Thunder Prophet/Geoffrey/Jailer*); Sue Jones-Davis (*Judith, a Beautiful Revolutionary*); John Young (*Matthias, a Stonee*); Bernard McKenna (*Official Stoners' Helper/*

MONTY PYTHON'S LIFE OF BRIAN

MONTY PYTHON'S LIFE OF BRIAN: Graham Chapman (kneeling), John Cleese (second from right), and Michael Palin (right).

Revolutionaries and Masked Commandos/Giggling Guard/Parvus, a Centurion); Andrew MacLachlan (*Another Official Stoners' Helper/Revolutionaries and Masked Commandos/Giggling Guard*); Neil Innes (*A Weedy Samaritan at the Forum*); Chris Langham (*Revolutionaries and Masked Commandos/Giggling Guard/ Alfonso*); John Case (*Pilate's Wife*); Charles Knode (*Passerby*); Spike Milligan (*Spike*); George Harrison (*Mr. Papadopoulis*).

COMMENTARY

Monty Python, the irreverent British satirical troupe, was responsible for *Life of Brian*, which presented the tale of a bumbling, reluctant Messiah (Graham Chapman) whose life runs parallel to that of Jesus Christ (Ken Colley). This scattershot comedy pulls no punches in its

193

MONTY PYTHON'S LIFE OF BRIAN: **Michael Palin as Pilate, flanked by John Cleese (left) and Graham Chapman.**

MONTY PYTHON'S LIFE OF BRIAN: Graham Chapman and Terry Jones.

biting attack on religious hypocrisy, and although the jokes sometimes go too far, there is cogent truth in some of the movie's observations about society's frequent corruption of religion. As an example, when Jesus delivers the Sermon on the Mount, the audience in the distance, unable to hear him, misinterprets his pronouncements, and fighting erupts in its midst.

In one of the film's most notorious scenes, Chapman, crucified with several other martyrs, sings "Always Look on the Bright Side of Life" while the victims sway in time to the music!

REVIEWS

. . . Should prove as appetizing to hardcore fans of the British comedy troupe as was *Monty Python and the Holy Grail*.

Variety

This is no gentle spoof, no good-natured satire of cherished beliefs. The Pythons' assault on religion is as intense as their attack on romantic chivalry in *Monty Python and the Holy Grail*.

Time

The film might also be taken seriously as an attempt to demystify Christ and religious fanaticism, while it unsuccessfully sends up the kind of reverent, choir-laden, star-studded gospel dramatisations habitually perpetrated by the cinema industry on behalf of God and Mammon.

Monthly Film Bulletin

JESUS

1979 Warner Bros.

CREDITS

Directors: Peter Sykes, John Kirsh; *Producer:* John Heyman; *Screenplay:* Barnet Fishbein; *Costumes:* Rochelle Zaltzman. *Photographed in color. Running Time:* 117 minutes.

CAST

Brian Deacon played *Jesus* in a cast that included: Rivka Noiman (*Mary*); Yossef Shiloah (*Joseph*); Niko Nital (*Simon Peter*); Gadi Rol (*Andrew*); Itzhak Ne'eman (*James*); Shmuel Tal (*John*), Kobi Assaf (*Philip*); Michael Varshaviak (*Bartholomew*); Mosko Alkalai (*Matthew*); Nisim Gerama (*Thomas*); Leonid Weinstein (*James, Son of Alphaeus*); Rafi Milo (*Simon Zelotes*); David Goldberg (*Judas, Son of James*); Eli Danker (*Judas Iscariot*); Eli Cohen (*John the Baptist*); Talia Shapira (*Mary Magdalene*); Richard Peterson (*Herod*); Miki Mfir (*Simon the Pharisee*); Peter Frye (*Pontius Pilate*); Alexander Scourby (*Narrator*).

COMMENTARY

A faithful adaptation of Christ's life as presented in the Gospel of Luke, this picture was filmed by the Genesis Project, a religious production company headed by John Heyman, the movie's producer. In a publicity statement, Heyman declared: "What we have made is a first century docudrama. When you see Christ in this film, you can believe that he is a man who spent eighteen years in a carpenter's shop before he started his ministry. He is a man who can smile and laugh and share his emotions with people." Although Brian Deacon's performance as Jesus was good and the film's producers were sincere, *Jesus* emerged as lacking in dramatic intensity and rushed through Christ's life in a simplified narrative that left little room for emotional depth and directorial nuance. The film was narrated by Alexander Scourby, who recorded *The Living Bible*.

REVIEWS

Jesus, clearly made by the devout principally for the already converted, is a *Classic Comics* version of the oft-told tale.

Variety

The movie is . . . mercifully spared the hype that commercial filmmakers usually inflict on biographies of Christ.

Time

Religiously faithful to the text, *Jesus* is a redundant plod through the greatest story ever

JESUS: Three phases in Jesus's life are represented in this specially posed publicity photo: Brian Deacon as the adult Jesus, Jonathan King (right) as the twelve-year-old Jesus, and an infant belonging to one of the film's extras as the newborn Jesus.

JESUS: The Crucifixion.

JESUS: Brian Deacon (center) performs the miracle of the loaves and fishes.

JESUS: Brian Deacon (left) as Jesus, with Eli Denker as Judas.

JESUS: From left: Mary Magdalene (Dalia Shapira), James (Babi Neeman), and
Peter (Niko Mitai) listen to the parables of Jesus (Brian Deacon).

JESUS: Brian Deacon.

told. Our Redeemer is characterized as a foot-loose proto-hippy who delivers the Sermon on the Mount during an informal walkabout. . . . Performances and direction . . . are sufficiently bland to ensure that the film never quite gets stuck in the kitsch mire of the more extravagant biblical epics.

Monthly Film Bulletin

MORE FILMS OF THE 1970s

The Christ of the Ocean (Izaro Films, 1971) was a low-budget Spanish-Italian coproduction reportedly based on a story by Anatole France. A young boy, orphaned by his guardian, a fisherman, discovers a life-size crucifix floating in the ocean. The salvaged crucifix is put on display in the local church, but the figure of Christ detaches itself from the cross and is found lying on the floor one morning. A mysterious stranger then appears and comforts the boy over the loss of his guardian, and eventually reunites the youngster with his long-lost mother. The stranger vanishes as suddenly as he appeared, with the possibility that he was Jesus Christ strongly inferred.

JESUS: The Crucifixion.

A pretentious 1972 satire directed by Robert Downey, *Greaser's Palace* (Cinema 5) follows Jesus Christ (Allan Arbus) as he parachutes into a nineteenth-century Western town dressed in a 1940s zoot suit and performs miracles (the resurrection of a gunfighter) as the final days of his life are reenacted. Undermined by dense symbolism and humorless gags, the film was deservedly lambasted by critics.

The Master and Margherite (Euro International, 1972), a Yugoslavian-Italian coproduction directed by Aleksander Petrovic, is set in Moscow during 1925, and focuses on Satan (Alain Cuny). Disguised as Woland, a practitioner of black magic, Satan is intent on creating havoc as a playwright (Ugo Tognazzi) attempts to mount a stage production of *Pontius Pilate*. Radomir Reljic plays Jesus in this allegory.

A new version of *Salomé*, released by Ital Noleggio Films, was imported from Italy in 1972. Directed by Carmelo Bené and featuring Donyale Luna in the starring role, the picture was the most offensive version of the story yet filmed, containing gratuitous violence and explicit nudity. As *Variety* noted in its review: "Single sequence of note is Bené's striking mocking vision of Christ nailing himself to the cross, unable to finish the job."

The Trial of Jesus (Aldebaran Films, 1974) was a minor allegory from Spain, directed by José Saenz de Heredia. The main story was contemporary, but a flashback to Jesus's trial was included.

Another screen allegory was *The Last Supper* (Tricontinental, 1978), produced in Cuba. It told of black workers forced to reenact the Last Supper by their tyrannical employer. Tomas Gutierrez directed.

Director Roberto Rossellini's *The Messiah* (De Rance, 1978), an Italian production, was released after his death. In its review of May 10, 1978, *Variety* wrote: "It is an inspiring work, a film by a religious man, and at all times stunning as well as shocking. There are the elaborate camera movements and zooms so much a part of Rossellini's work which had been criticized in later years as distracting. It works elegantly here."

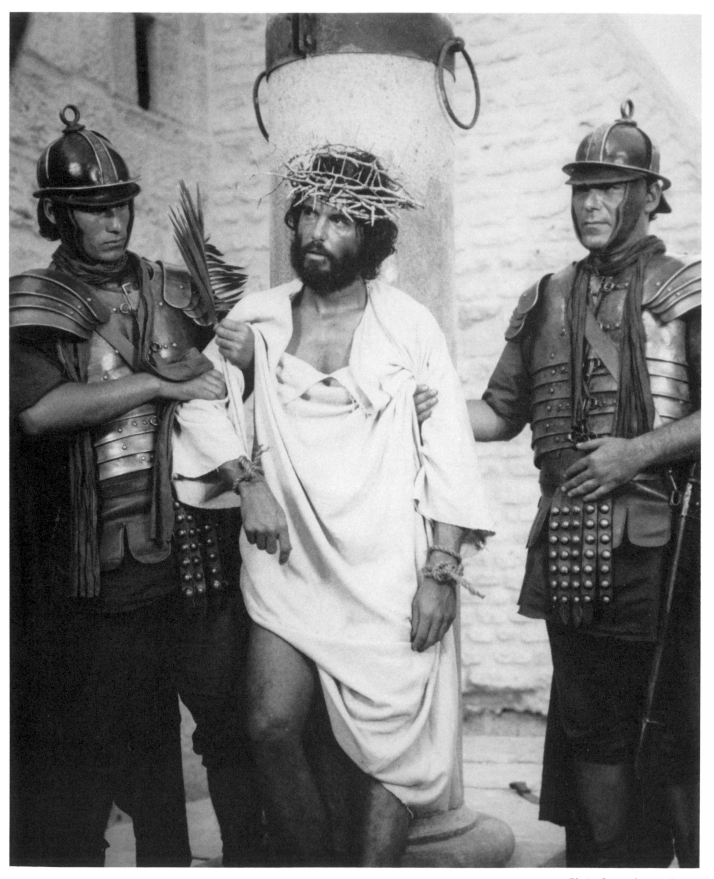

THE DAY CHRIST DIED: Chris Sarandon as Jesus.

CHAPTER 8

THE NINETEEN EIGHTIES

THE DAY CHRIST DIED

*1980 Martin Manulis Productions/
20th Century-Fox TV for CBS*

CREDITS

Director: James Cellan Jones; *Producer:* Martin Manulis; *Associate Producer:* Ted Butcher; *Screenplay:* James Lee Barrett, Edward Anhalt (*based on the book by* Jim Bishop); *Photography* (*color*): Franco Di Giacomo; *Music:* Laurence Rosenthal; *Film Editor:* Barry Peters; *Art Director:* Gianni Quaranta; *Costumes:* Dada Scaligeri; *Religious Advisor:* Rev. Terrance A. Sweeney; *Consultants:* Dr. Eugene J. Fisher; Rev. Patrick J. Sullivan. *Running Time:* 180 minutes.

CAST

Chris Sarandon played *Jesus* in a cast that included: Colin Blakely (*Caiaphas*); Keith Michell (*Pontius Pilate*); Jonathan Pryce (*King Herod*); Barrie Houghton (*Judas*); Jay O. Sanders (*Peter*); Eleanor Bron (*Mary*); Tim Pigott-Smith (*Tullius*); Delia Boccardo (*Mary Magdalene*); Hope Lange (*Claudia*); Oliver Cotton (*John*); Gordon Gostelow (*Nicodemus*); Harold Goldblatt (*Annas*); Gary Brown (*Aaron*); Leonard Maguire (*The Demoniac*); Marne Maitland (*Jacob*); Tony Vogel (*First Temple Guard*); Brian Coburn (*James*);
Emma Jacobs (*Leliah*); Ralph Arliss (*Matthew*); Anna Nogara (*Ruth*); Dov Gottesfeld (*Andrew*); Anthony Langdon, Donal O'Brien (*Roman Soldiers*); Rodd Dana (*Abenadar*); John Savident (*Aide to Herod*); Thomas Milian, Jr. (*Mark*); Joseph Murphy, Ted Rusoff (*Temple Guards*); Charles Boromel (*Second Witness*); Donald Hodson (*Joseph of Arimethea*); Veronica Welles (*Sara*); Leonardo Treviglio (*Thomas*); Cyrus Elisa (*Herod's Messenger*); Fabrizio Jovine (*Phillip*); Nando Paone (*Thaddeus*); Samuele Cerri (*Nathaniel*); Marie-Cristine Dunham (*Deborah*); Jean-Paul Boucher (*James the Younger*); Mattia Machiavelli (*Simon*).

COMMENTARY

The Day Christ Died offered a "revisionist" view of Jesus as a helpless pawn of the Roman government and the religious leaders of Jerusalem, intentionally deemphasizing Jesus's divinity. The creators of this film, adapted from Jim Bishop's best-seller, were apparently unsure of exactly what they wanted to do; as a result of their diffused efforts, the picture fails both as religious commentary and as historical drama. Although it is certainly objectionable from a religious point of view, and CBS initially

IN SEARCH OF HISTORIC JESUS: John Rubinstein.

feared that the film's broadcast would stir controversy, the expected protest never materialized. The script by Edward Anhalt and James Lee Barrett was so confused and bland that it stirred little emotion, and Chris Sarandon's performance as Jesus, though sincere, was so compromised by mediocre writing that the film was simply ignored by the public. In comparison to director Franco Zeffirelli's excellent *Jesus of Nazareth*, broadcast only a couple of years before, *The Day Christ Died* seems especially weak.

REVIEWS

Mr. Sarandon . . . conveys no impression of internal strength, let alone divine paternity.

New York Times

Historical authenticity—costumes, torches, religious ceremonies—and today's acting styles with deviations from Biblical characters' personalities and actions as accepted over the years give the Martin Manulis production about the last day of Christ on earth a flat, uncommitted view. Somewhere along the line, someone decided rhetoric and naturalism were good replacements for reverence and true drama; they aren't . . . . Chris Sarandon plays Jesus as a stern man determined to fulfill the prophesies, a man not afraid to say He doesn't want to die but confident of His mission. . . . Sarandon offers earnestness in place of warmth.

Variety

IN SEARCH OF HISTORIC JESUS

1980 Sunn Classics

CREDITS

Director: Henning Schellerup; *Producers:* Charles E. Sellier, Jr., James L. Conway; *Screenplay:* Marvin Wald (*based on the book by* Lee Roddy *and* Charles E. Sellier, Jr.); *Photography (Technicolor):* Paul Hipp; *Music:* Bob Summers; *Film Editor:* Kendall S. Rase; *Production Designer:* Paul Staheli; *Art Direction:* Doug Vandergrift; *Set Designer:* Randy Staheli; *Costumes:* Julie Staheli; *Special Effects:* John Carter. *Running Time:* 91 minutes.

CAST

John Rubinstein played *Jesus* in a cast that included: *John Anderson (Caiaphas);* Nehemiah Persoff (*Herod Antipas*); Brad Crandall (*Narrator*); Andrew Bloch (*John*); Morgan Brittany (*Mary*); Walter Brooke (*Joseph*); Annette Charles (*Mary Magdalene*); Royal Dano (*Prophet*); Anthony DeLongis (*Peter*); Lawrence Dobkin (*Pontius Pilate*); David Opatoshu (*Herod*); Richard Carlyle (*Astrologer*); Jeffrey Druce (*Thomas*); WITH John Hoyt, Stanley Kamel, Al Ruscio, Harvey Solin, Richard Alfieri, Robert Bonvento, Travis DeCastro, Steve DeFrance, John Hansen, Jack Ingersoll, Richard Jury, Marty McGreal.

COMMENTARY

A pseudo-documentary, *In Search of Historic Jesus* examines Jesus as an historical figure and asks questions like: Was Jesus the Son of God? Did he work miracles? All the while, John Rubinstein portrays Christ in cheaply filmed scenes illustrating the narration.

The film's premise was loosely constructed around the mystery of the Shroud of Turin, a burial garment believed by many to have covered Jesus after his entombment following the Crucifixion. Actor/composer John Rubinstein, son of piano virtuoso Artur Rubinstein, was a visually impressive Jesus, but was defeated by the low-budget nature of the production. Veteran character actor Nehemiah Persoff was also wasted in the role of Herod Antipas.

At this time Sunn Classics was successfully producing cheap pseudo-documentaries such as this on a variety of subjects. The company then employed an exhibition technique known as "four walling"—renting a number of theaters outright on a regional basis for the picture's brief local run (with all ticket sales going to the distributor), and heavily promoting the film with a saturation media campaign often misrepresenting the product and invariably leaving moviegoers dissatisfied after they had paid to see the picture. *In Search of Historic Jesus* was no better or worse than the general run of the lot.

REVIEW

Some may consider such an exercise in pictorialized rhetoric as harmless; others may see exploitation of the mass audience in a deplorable sense. The film's "theology" will not bear scrutiny.

Variety

JE VOUS SALUE, MARIE

(Hail, Mary)

France/Switzerland

1985 Sara Films/Pegase Films/ JLG Films/Gaumont

CREDITS

Writer/Director: Jean-Luc Godard; *Producers:* Philippe Malignon, Francois Pelissier; *Photography (color):* Jean-Bernard Menoud, Jacques Frimann; *Music:* Johann Sebastian Bach, Anton Dvořák, John Coltrane.

CAST

Malachi Jara Kohan played *Jesus* in a cast that included: Myriem Roussel (*Mary*); Thierry Rode (*Joseph*); Philippe Lacoste (*The Angel*); Juliette Binoche (*Juliette*); Manon Anderson (*Little Girl*); Dick (*Arthur*); Johann Leysen (*Professor*); Anne Gauthier (*Eva*).

COMMENTARY

Provocative French film auteur Jean-Luc Godard's *Hail, Mary* caused a storm of controversy over its modernization of the Annunciation, depicting Mary (Myriem Roussel) as a

HAIL, MARY: Thierry Lacoste, Myriem Roussel (background), and Malachi Jara Kohan (foreground) as Jesus.

virginal girl who pumps gas at a service station and Joseph (Thierry Rode) as a taxi driver. The film examines the conflict that develops as the bewildered young couple struggles to accept and understand the Immaculate Conception and Virgin Birth of Mary's son (Malachi Jara Kohan). Although it shocked many with its contemporary setting, profane language, and frequent (though tasteful) nude scenes of Roussel, *Hail, Mary* is undeniably a sincere examination of faith, and ultimately a reaffirmation of that faith.

Perhaps director-scenarist Godard, who chose such an unconventional overall approach at the outset, should have extended his thinking to the names of his main characters. If they had been called anything except Mary, Joseph, and Jesus, the film's point could have been made just as well, and the tumultuous protests that greeted its initial screenings avoided.

HAIL, MARY: Myriem Roussel as Mary.

It's . . . about the demands of faith, which in this time of cynicism, may be the most truly controversial aspect of the movie.

New York Times

The film's bark is worse than its bite. Indeed, there is actually some genuine religious feeling in the movie. . .

Commonweal

It is entirely appropriate that Godard should have returned to the "sources" of narrative, the Bible, for his modern-day account of the immaculate conception. The metaphorical element of Godard's early storytelling has been increasingly drained from his recent films.

Monthly Film Bulletin

THE SEVENTH SIGN

1988 Tri-Star

CREDITS

Director: Carl Schultz; *Producers:* Ted Field, Robert W. Cort; *Screenplay:* W. W. Wicket (Ellen Green),

THE SEVENTH SIGN: Jurgen Prochnow.

George Kaplan (Clifford Green); *Photography (Panavision, Technicolor)*: Juan Ruiz Anchia; *Music*: Jack Nitzsche; *Lyrics*: David Kurt; *Film Editor*: Caroline Biggerstaff; *Production Design*: Stephen Marsh; *Art Direction*: Francesca Bartoccini; *Special Effects*: Ray Svedin, Hans Metz; *Costumes*: Durinda Rice Wood; *Special Makeup Effects*: Robert Ryan, Greg Nelson, Kevin Yeager, Craig Reardon. *Running Time*: 97 minutes.

CAST

Jurgen Prochnow played *Jesus/David* in a cast that included: Demi Moore (*Abby Quinn*); Michael Biehn (*Russell Quinn*); Peter Friedman (*Father Lucci*); Manny Jacobs (*Avi*); John Taylor (*Jimmy Zaragoza*); Lee Garlington (*Dr. Inness*); Akosua Busia (*Penny*); Harry W. Basil (*Kid's Korner Salesman*); Arnold Johnson (*Janitor*); John Walcutt (*Novitiate*); Michael Laskin (*Israeli Colonel*); Hugo L. Stranger (*Old Priest*); Patricia Allison (*Administrator*); Ian Buchanan (*Meteorologist*); Glenn Edwards, Robin Groth, Dick Spangler (*Newscasters*); Darwyn Carson, Harry Bartron, Dale Butcher, Dorothy Sinclair, Larry Eisenberg (*Reporters*); Lisa Hestrin, Christine Carman, Irene Fernicola, Karen Shaver, Kathryn Miller, Cornelia Whitcomb, Yuri Ogawa (*Nurses*); Mariko Tse (*Private Nurse*); Adam Nelson, David King (*Paramedics*); Sonny Santiago (*Medical Technician*); Fredric Arnold (*Surgeon*); Rabbi Baruch Cohon (*Cantor*); Leonard Cimino (*Head Cardinal*); Richard Devon (*Second Cardinal*); Rabbi William Kramer (*Rabbi Ornstein*); Blanche Rubin (*Mrs. Ornstein*); John Heard (*Reverend*); Joe Mays (*Motel Clerk*); Jane Frances (*Game Show Woman*); Robert Herron, J. N. Roberts, Hank Calia, Gary Epper, John Sherwood (*Jimmy's Guards*).

COMMENTARY

The Seventh Sign features a Christ-like figure (Jurgen Prochnow) in an allegorical horror-fantasy centering on the coming Apocalypse, heralded by the fulfillment of several prophesied biblical disasters. The Prochnow character, called David, wanders the earth instigating seven biblical disasters which will eventually lead to the foretold Apocalypse. Arriving in Venice, California, David rents a garage apartment from a young pregnant woman, Abby Quinn (Demi Moore), intending to use her unborn child in order to fulfill the "Seventh Sign," the stillbirth of a baby without a soul.

David's activities are being followed by the mysterious Father Lucci (Peter Friedman), while Abby's husband Russell (Michael Biehn), a lawyer, is attempting to save a client from the death penalty.

These seemingly unrelated plot elements intertwine when it is revealed that, in a previous life, Abby Quinn was offered the chance to exchange her own life for Christ's at the Crucifixion, and that Father Lucci was the Roman soldier then present who made the offer. David finally reveals that he can prevent the Apocalypse in exchange for Abby's life, and tells her that she can also save her baby's life if she stops the execution of her husband's client, a mentally retarded young man convicted of murder. Father Lucci must wander through eternity if the Apocalypse does not occur, and the film ends with Abby battling him to prevent the Apocalypse and attempting to save her husband's client from the death penalty.

Unbelievably convoluted and more than a little silly, *The Seventh Sign* does feature good performances and excellent Panavision photography by Juan Ruiz Anchia, featuring dramatic lighting effects. The script was by Ellen and Clifford Green, credited under the pseudonyms W. W. Wicket and George Kaplan.

REVIEWS

If the seventh sign of the Apocalypse is anything like the film *The Seventh Sign*, the world needn't worry. There's about two minutes of suspense with the rest a fairly tame dramatization of revelations from the Bible. It's doubtful this will excite film audiences much.

Variety

It's clear that the writers have taken some liberties with their source material, so many, in fact, that the film's theology is even more opaque than Revelation's revelations.

New York Times

THE LAST TEMPTATION OF CHRIST

1988 Universal

CREDITS

Director: Martin Scorsese; *Executive Producer:* Harry Ufland; *Producer:* Barbara De Fina; *Screenplay:* Paul Schrader (*based on the novel by* Nikos Kazantzakis; *Photography (Technicolor):* Michael Ballhaus; *Music:* Peter Gabriel; *Film Editor:* Thelma Schoonmaker; *Production Design:* John Beard; *Art Director:* Andrew Sanders; *Set Decorator:* Giorgio Desideri; *Costumes:* Jean-Pierre Delifer; *Choreography:* Lachen Zinoune; *Special Effects:* Dino Galliano, Iginio Fiorentini; *Makeup:* Manilo Rocchetti; *Running Time:* 164 minutes.

CAST

Willem Dafoe played *Jesus* in a cast that included: Harvey Keitel (*Judas Iscariot*); Barbara Hershey (*Mary Magdalene*); Harry Dean Stanton (*Saul/Paul*); David Bowie (*Pontius Pilate*); Verna Bloom (*Mary, Mother of Jesus*); André Gregory (*John the Baptist*); Juliette Caton (*Girl Angel*); Roberts Blossom (*Aged Master*); Irvin Kershner (*Zebedee*); Gary Basaraba (*Andrew, Apostle*); Victor Argo (*Peter, Apostle*); Michael Been (*John, Apostle*); Paul Herman (*Phillip, Apostle*); John Lurie (*James, Apostle*); Leo Burmester (*Nathaniel, Apostle*); Alan Rosenberg (*Thomas, Apostle*); Tomas Arana (*Lazarus*); Nehemiah Persoff (*Rabbi*); Barry Miller (*Jeroboam*); Paul Greco (*Zealot*); Steven Shill (*Centurion*); Russell Case, Mary Seller, Donna Marie (*People at Sermon*); Mohamed Mabsout, Ahmed Nacir, Mokhtar Salouf, Mahamed Ait Fdil Ahmed (*Other Apostles*); Peggy Gormley (*Martha, Sister of Lazarus*); Randy Danson (*Mary, Sister of Lazarus*); Robert Spafford (*Man at Wedding*); Doris von Thury (*Woman with Mary, Mother of Jesus*); Del Russel (*Money Changer*); Donald Hodson (*Saducee*); Peter Berling (*Beggar*); Penny Brown, Gabi Ford, Dale Wyatt, Domenico Fiore, Tomas Arana, Ted Rusoff, Leo Damian, Robert Laconi, Jonathon Zhivago, Illeana Douglas, David Sharp (*People in Crowd*); Khalid Benghrib, Redouane Farhane, Fabienne Panchiatili, Naima Skikes, Souad Rahal, Otmane Chbani Idrissi, Jamal Belkhayat (*Dancers*); Leo Marks (*Voice of the Devil*).

COMMENTARY

Shot in Morocco on a small budget of $6.5 million, director Martin Scorsese's *The Last Temptation of Christ* was released amidst a firestorm of controversy. Adapted from the novel by Nikos Kazantzakis (initially brought to Scorsese's attention in 1972 by actress Barbara Hershey, who plays Mary Magdalene here), the film seeks to examine, and ultimately reaffirm, Jesus's faith in his own divinity by exploring his doubts and indecisions about himself and his destiny. This theme is introduced immediately and crystalizes in the movie's final third, when a crucified Jesus is given a reprieve from his death by a young female angel, who tells Christ that God feels he has suffered enough. Leading Jesus from the cross into an idyllic alternate life, the angel guides him as he weds Mary Magdalene and lives happily to old age, finally realizing on his deathbed that he has, in fact, renounced God and his own fate. Jesus, horrified, struggles to emerge from this dream world, realizing that the beautiful "angel" is really an agent of Satan. He returns to the cross, where only a moment has passed in reality, and he accepts his destiny, overcoming the "last temptation." His Resurrection is then visualized in a burst of multicolored light.

As *Time* critic Richard Corliss noted in his appraisal: "Martin Scorsese's first achievement in *The Last Temptation of Christ* is to strip the biblical epic of its encrusted sanctimony and show biz. . . . By jolting the viewer to reconsider Hollywood's calcified stereotypes of the New Testament, Scorsese wants to restore the immediacy of that time, the stern wonder of that land, the thrilling threat of meeting the Messiah on the mean streets of Jerusalem." The public outcry against the movie was far more widespread and volatile than any previous criticism directed against a Hollywood religious film, and the picture's concluding segment, as described above, was responsible for drawing the most ire from Scorsese's accusers, most of whom had not seen the film and had no idea at all that the offending events occurred in a *fantasy* sequence. Corliss continued in his *Time* review: "Any Jesus film with sex and violence is bound to roil the faithful. For Scorsese, though, these elements are bold colors on the canvas, images of the life Jesus must renounce and redeem. The sex scene (in

which Barbara Hershey's Mary Magdalene entertains some customers) exposes a strong woman's degradation more than it does her flesh. And the film's carnage is emetic, not exploitative. The crowning with thorns, the scourging at the pillar, the agonized trudge up Calvary show what Jesus suffered and why."

Indeed, the flaws in *The Last Temptation of Christ* are more stylistic than theological. The film's middle portion is a fairly straightforward recounting of Christ's life, and Scorsese is directorially weakest in these portions, relying on facile devices like quick dissolves to multiply Jesus's Disciples as he gains followers. Scenarist Paul Schrader's dialogue is also an irritant at times, unwisely employing contemporary phrasing and speech patterns in an attempt to make the characters seem more immediate. Although quite good in a role that, as interpreted here, is even more complicated

THE LAST TEMPTATION OF CHRIST: Willem Dafoe.

than usual, Willem Dafoe seems too much of a whining neurotic in the film's early scenes, and some passages, like the confrontation with a talking lion during Jesus's forty days and nights in the desert, border on the ridiculous. But *The Last Temptation of Christ*, despite these flaws and the fundamentalist outrage expressed toward the film and Scorsese, must rank as one of the most gripping and effective screen adaptations of Christ's story.

REVIEWS

Although the film remains engrossing throughout, some scenes bog down a bit in too much talk, and there are occasional jarring colloquialisms.

Variety

Though the choices that shape this exceptionally ambitious, deeply troubling and, at

THE LAST TEMPTATION OF CHRIST: Barbara Hershey as Mary Magdalene.

THE LAST TEMPTATION OF CHRIST: Clockwise: David Bowie (as Pontius Pilate), Verna Bloom (as the Virgin Mary), Harry Dean Stanton (as Saul/Paul), and André Gregory (as John the Baptist).

infrequent moments, genuinely transcendent film are often contradictory, they create an extra dimension. Mr. Scorsese's evident struggle with this material becomes as palpable as the story depicted on the screen.

New York Times

JESUS OF MONTREAL

Canada/France

*1989 Max Films International/
Gerard Mital Productions*

CREDITS

Writer/Director: Denys Arcand; *Producers:* Roger Frappier, Pierre Gendron; *Photography* (*color*): Guy Dufaux; *Music:* Yves Laferriére; *Film Editor:* Isabelle Dedieu; *Production Design:* Francois Séguin; *Sound:* Patrick Rousseau. *Running Time:* 120 minutes.

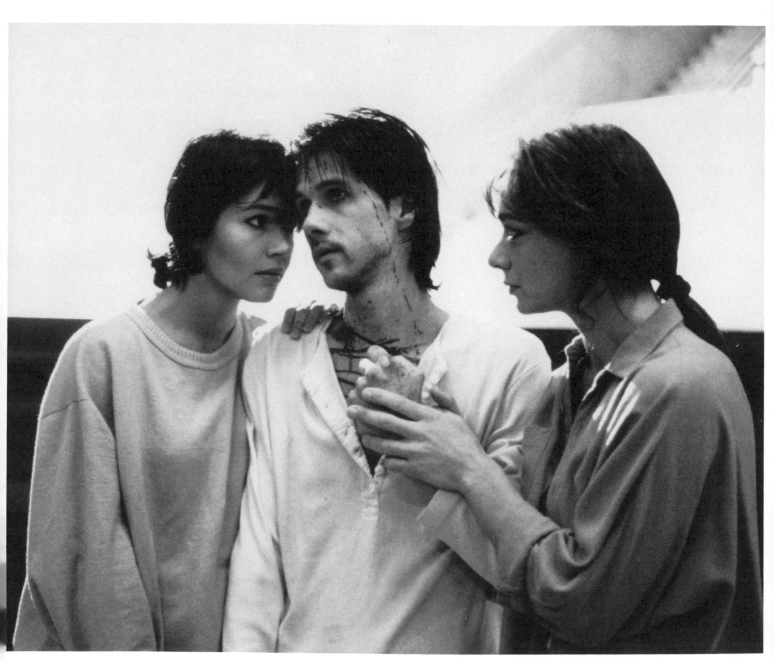

JESUS OF MONTREAL: Catherine Wilkening (left), Lothaire Bluteau, and Johane-Marie Tremblay.

CAST

Lothaire Bluteau (*Daniel*); Catherine Wilkening (*Mireille*); Johanne-Marie Tremblay (*Constance*); Rémy Girard (*Martin*); Robert Lepage (*René*); Gilles Pelletier (*Father Leclerc*); Yves Jacques (*Richard Cardinal*); Denys Arcand (*The Judge*).

COMMENTARY

A brilliant allegory, *Jesus of Montreal* examines the dilemma facing Daniel (Lothaire Bluteau), a struggling young actor who earns a living overdubbing voices in pornographic films, when he is asked by his local priest to write and direct a passion play and take the role of Jesus. His portrayal begins to affect him, as well as his friends and coworkers, when his life begins to mirror the role he is playing. Events in Daniel's life are used by writer/director Arcand to parallel Jesus's teachings, such as Daniel's growing contempt for materialism, expressed when he destroys a roomful of video equipment. The hypocrisy of the story's religious leaders is also underlined when the priest, who had prompted Daniel to "modernize" the Passion Play in order to draw a larger audience, does an abrupt about face and objects to the radical but sincere changes Daniel has made.

Although Arcand's film is often satiric, it is undeniably serious in theme, expressing the genuine need for spiritual fulfillment in a corrupt modern society, and the potential achievement of that spiritual fulfillment through pure artistic expression.

REVIEWS

Wickedly funny, searingly honest satire on the way the message of Jesus Christ has been distorted through history.

Variety

Even if Arcand departs from the Bible, or oversecularizes it, he does try to bring alive some of its central values and idealism.

America

A CHILD CALLED JESUS

1989 Leone Film (Italy)/Tribune Entertainment

CREDITS

Director: Franco Rossi; *Executive Producer:* Ridha Turki; *Producers:* Elio Scardamaglia, Francesco Scardamaglia; *Teleplay:* Vittorio Bonicelli, Francesco Scardamaglia, Franco Rossi; *Photography (color):* Gianfranco Transuto; *Music:* Pero Piccioni; *Film Editors:* Giorgio Serrallonga, Domenico Varone; *Production Design:* Enrico Fiorentini; *Sound:* Hechim Joulak, Riadh Thabet; *Head of Production:* Tarak Harbi; *Makeup:* Fatma Jaziri; *Hairdresser:* Essia Baaziz; *Special Effects:* Ditta Giovani Corridori. *English Language Version—Dialogue/Teleplay:* Edward Mannix; *Film Editor:* Ron Heidt. *Running Time:* 240 minutes (telecast in two parts).

CAST

Allessandro Gassman played *Jesus* (as an adult) in a cast that included: Matteo Bellina (*Young Jesus*); Pierre Clementi (*Sefir*); Bekim Fehmiu (*Joseph*); Carmen San Martin (*Mary*); Franco Interlenghi (*Titus Rufus*); Franco Citti (*The Shepherd*); Frederick Darie (*Elijah*); Duta Sec (*The Hermit*); Kamel Touati (*Omar*); Habdellatif Hamrouni (*Semira*); Fethi Hadroui (*Khella*); Brahim Mastoura (*Gad*); Fatma Harbi (*Esther*); Kauther Bardi (*The Bride*); Hatm Hayeb (*The Groom*); Bechir Drosi (*Roman Bureaucrat*); Hlima Droud (*Mother of the Leper*); Moncef Bel Jadj Xahia (*The Teacher*); Salh Miled (*Head of the Caravan*); Ahmad Tounsi (*The Cantor*); Fatma Saidane (*The Miraculously Healed*); Haffeb Semlali (*King Herod*).

COMMENTARY

This Italian made-for-TV production (shot mainly in Tunisia) was originally telecast in Italy, Germany, and France before being syndicated in America by Tribune Entertainment. Broadcast in two two-hour segments, it begins with the birth of Jesus to Mary and Joseph, and follows Jesus through his early years as Sefir, an evil servant of King Herod, attempts to murder Jesus and fulfill Herod's edict that all male children born in Bethlehem during the last three years must die. Joseph flees with his family to Alexandria, where he finds work as a shipyard carpenter, and is nearly killed when Sefir follows them and sets fire to the shipyard. Mary and Joseph are captured by Roman sol-

A CHILD CALLED JESUS: Joseph (Bekim Fehmiu) and Mary (Maria Del Carmen San Martin) begin an arduous trek through the desert with young Jesus (Matteo Bellina).

diers, and then turned over to Sefir, who leads them away, forcing the mother and child to walk behind his horse through the blistering desert sands. After days of this torment, young Jesus performs a miracle when he cures a leper, and this convinces Sefir to renounce Herod's command and free Mary and Jesus, who are eventually reunited with Joseph.

Although flawed somewhat by clumsy dubbing, *A Child Called Jesus* is well-produced, with beautiful photography. The film, directed by Franco Rossi, who earlier had made the TV version of *Quo Vadis?*, won an International Emmy Award and received favorable consensus from the Vatican. After it earned high ratings in both Europe and America, a sequel was announced for future production.

REVIEWS

Veteran movie director Franco Rossi has succeeded in dramatizing a story of The Redeemer's childhood without being cloyingly pious nor annoyingly saccharine. It may not suit every taste or one's personal view of the Holy Family, but its visualization has a sense of mystery and the power of the divine . . . Noteworthy too are the many scenes demonstrating the Jewish identity of the Holy Family, an aspect of the production which quite naturally establishes the bridge between the Old Testament and the beginning of the New.

Catholic News Service

Italian production centering on 7-year-old Jesus and his family's exodus from Bethlehem would take more than 40 days and nights to drum up interest. Show's poor dubbing, amateurish acting and snail's-pace direction are just a few of its flaws. . . . Jesus is haunted by visions of his own death on the cross, but there is little else that gives evidence of his divinity.

Variety

A CHILD CALLED JESUS: **The Crucifixion.**

A CHILD CALLED JESUS: Matteo Bellina in the title role.

MORE FILMS OF THE 1980s

History of the World, Part I (20th Century-Fox), a forced, uneven, occasionally profane epic 1981 comedy directed by Mel Brooks, contained a scene in which Brooks played a waiter at the Last Supper, with Leonardo Da Vinci (Art Metrano) painting the scene and including Brooks, leering over the shoulder of Jesus (John Hurt), in the finished work.

The made-for-tv *Peter and Paul,* directed by Robert Day and starring Robert Foxworth (Peter) and Anthony Hopkins (Paul), appeared in 1981, with a cast that also included Raymond Burr, Herbert Lom, José Ferrer, Eddie Albert, and Jean Peters. *Variety* called it, "Reverential, respectful, cautious, and mostly plodding."

The Fourth Wise Man, a 1985 made-for-tv movie, starred Martin Sheen as the fictional title character who is separated from his three traveling companions, only to be eventually reunited with them at Jesus's Crucifixion.

An unexpected television remake of *Quo Vadis?* produced in Italy and directed by Franco Rossi, was seen on cable in the U.S. in 1985. However, the cast—including Francisco Quinn (Anthony's son) in the Robert Taylor role, along with an international roster ranging from Austria's Klaus Maria Brandauer as Nero, to America's Frederic Forrest and Cristina Raines, to Italy's Gabriele Ferzetti and Massimo Girotti, to Sweden's Max Von Sydow—was undistinguished and the plodding, four-hour film made little impression.

Two new versions, both R-rated, of the Salomé story were also released in the 1980s; *Salomé* (Cannon, 1986), with Jo Champa in the title role, and controversial British director Ken Russell's *Salomé's Last Dance* (Vestron, 1988). Somewhat novel in its approach to the oft-filmed subject, Russell's adaptation depicted Oscar Wilde (Nickolas Grace) watching a performance of his play staged at a brothel. Imogen Millais-Scott played Salomé.

A Danish production, *The Return of Jesus Christ,* was announced in late 1989 by controversial filmmaker and painter Jens Joergen Thorsen, who had spent nearly two decades trying to get it before the cameras over the objections of both the government and religious groups because of proposed sex scenes (Jesus in the nude and with a woman terrorist). After many delays, the film opened in Copenhagen in spring 1992. (The original title of this film was to have been *The Many Faces of Jesus Christ,* and an alternate title was *The Many Loves of Jesus Christ.*)

APPENDIX

Following is a comprehensive list of actors who have portrayed Jesus Christ on film, and the films they appeared in, arranged chronologically. Excluded are voice-only performances and Christ-like figures in allegories.

Frank Russell	*The Passion Play of Oberammergau* (1897)
M. Normand	*The Life and Passion of Jesus Christ* (1908)
Charles Kent	*Though Your Sins Be as Scarlet* (1911)
Robert Henderson-Bland	*From the Manger to the Cross* (1913)
Frederick W. Huntley	*The Three Wise Men* (1913)
Sydney Ayres	*The Last Supper* (1914)
Hobart Bosworth	*Business Is Business* (1915)
George Fisher	*Civilization* (1916)
Howard Gaye	*Intolerance* (1916) and *Restitution* (1918)
Giovanni Pasquali	*Christus* (1917)
Halvard Hoff	*Leaves From Satan's Book* (1922)
Gregori Chmara	*I. N. R. I.* (1923)
Adolph Fassnacht	*The Passion Play* (1924)
H. B. Warner	*The King of Kings* (1927)
Philip Van Loan	*Jesus of Nazareth* (1928)
Robert Le Vignan	*Golgotha* (1935)
Luis Alcoriza	*Mary Magdalene* (1946)
Millard Coody	*The Lawton Story* (1949)
Charles P. Carr	*The Westminster Passion Play* (1951)
Robert Wilson	*I Beheld His Glory* (1952) and *Day of Triumph* (1954)
Jon Shepodd	*The Power of the Resurrection* (1958)
Claude Heater	*Ben-Hur* (1959)
Jeffrey Hunter	*King of Kings* (1961)
Roy Mangano	*Barabbas* (1962)
Max Von Sydow	*The Greatest Story Ever Told* (1965)

Luis Alvarez	*The Redeemer* (1965)
Enrique Irazoqui	*The Gospel According to St. Matthew* (1966)
John Drew Barrymore	*Pontius Pilate* (1967)
Bernard Verley	*The Milky Way* (1969)
George Figgs	*Multiple Maniacs* (1970)
Donald Sutherland	*Johnny Got His Gun* (1971)
Radomir Reljic	*The Master and Margherite* (1972)
Victor Garber	*Godspell* (1973)
Robert Elfstrom	*The Gospel Road* (1973)
Ted Neely	*Jesus Christ, Superstar* (1973)
Finn Tavbe	*I Saw Jesus Die* (1976)
Zalman King	*The Passover Plot* (1976)
Robert Powell	*Jesus of Nazareth* (1977)
Ken Colley	*Monty Python's Life of Brian* (1979)
Brian Deacon	*Jesus* (1979)
Chris Sarandon	*The Day Christ Died* (1980)
John Rubinstein	*In Search of Historic Jesus* (1980)
John Hurt	*History of the World, Part I* (1981)
Malachi Jara Kohan	*Hail, Mary* (1985)
Willem Dafoe	*The Last Temptation of Christ* (1988)
Matteo Bellina (Young Jesus), Alessandro Gassman (Adult Jesus)	*A Child Called Jesus* (1989)

FREE!

Citadel Film Series Catalog

From James Stewart to Moe Howard and The Three Stooges, Woody Allen to John Wayne, The Citadel Film Series is America's largest film book library.

Now with more than 125 titles in print, books in the series make perfect gifts—for a loved one, a friend, or yourself!

We'd like to send you, free of charge, our latest full-color catalog describing the Citadel Film Series in depth. To receive the catalog, call 1-800-447-BOOK or send your name and address to:

Citadel Film Series/Carol Publishing Group
Distribution Center B
120 Enterprise Avenue
Secaucus, New Jersey 07094

The titles you'll find in the catalog include:
The Films Of...

Alan Ladd	Elizabeth Taylor	Jeanette MacDonald and	Pictorial History of Sex
Alfred Hitchcock	Elvis Presley	Nelson Eddy	in Films
All Talking! All Singing!	Errol Flynn	Jewish Image in American	Pictorial History of War
All Dancing!	Federico Fellini	Films	Films
Anthony Quinn	The Fifties	Joan Crawford	Pictorial History of the
The Bad Guys	The Forties	John Garfield	Western Film
Barbara Stanwyck	Forgotten Films	John Huston	Rebels: The Rebel Hero
Barbra Streisand:	to Remember	John Wayne	in Films
The First Decade	Frank Sinatra	John Wayne Reference	Rita Hayworth
Barbra Streisand:	Fredric March	Book	Robert Redford
The Second Decade	Gary Cooper	John Wayne Scrapbook	Robert Taylor
Bela Lugosi	Gene Kelly	Judy Garland	Ronald Reagan
Bette Davis	Gina Lollobrigida	Katharine Hepburn	The Seventies
Bing Crosby	Ginger Rogers	Kirk Douglas	Sex in the Movies
Black Hollywood	Gloria Swanson	Lana Turner	Sci-Fi 2
Boris Karloff	Great Adventure Films	Laurel and Hardy	Sherlock Holmes
Bowery Boys	Great British Films	Lauren Bacall	Shirley MacLaine
Brigitte Bardot	Great French Films	Laurence Olivier	Shirley Temple
Burt Reynolds	Great German Films	Lost Films of the	The Sixties
Carole Lombard	Great Romantic Films	Fifties	Sophia Loren
Cary Grant	Great Science Fiction Films	Love in the Film	Spencer Tracy
Cecil B. DeMille	Great Spy Films	Mae West	Steve McQueen
Character People	Gregory Peck	Marilyn Monroe	Susan Hayward
Charles Bronson	Greta Garbo	Marlon Brando	Tarzan of the Movies
Charlie Chaplin	Harry Warren and the	Moe Howard and The	They Had Faces Then
Charlton Heston	Hollywood Musical	Three Stooges	The Thirties
Chevalier	Hedy Lamarr	Montgomery Clift	Those Glorious Glamour Years
Clark Gable	Hello! My Real Name Is	More Character People	Three Stooges Book of Scripts
Classics of the Gangster	Henry Fonda	More Classics of the	Three Stooges Book of Scripts,
Film	Hollywood Cheesecake:	Horror Film	Vol. 2
Classics of the Horror Film	60 Years of Leg Art	More Films of the '30s	The Twenties
Classics of the Silent Screen	Hollywood's Hollywood	Myrna Loy	20th Century Fox
Cliffhanger	Howard Hughes in Hollywood	Non-Western Films of	Warren Beatty
Clint Eastwood	Humphrey Bogart	John Ford	W. C. Fields
Curly: Biography of a	Ingrid Bergman	Norma Shearer	Western Films of John Ford
Superstooge	Jack Lemmon	Olivia de Havilland	West That Never Was
Detective in Film	Jack Nicholson	Paul Newman	William Holden
Dick Tracy	James Cagney	Paul Robeson	William Powell
Dustin Hoffman	James Stewart	Peter Lorre	Woody Allen
Early Classics of the	Jane Fonda	Pictorial History of Science	World War II
Foreign Film	Jayne Mansfield	Fiction Films	